T0121963

Sophocles

Ajax

A new translation and
commentary by Shomit Dutta

Introduction to the Greek Theatre
by P.E. Easterling

Series Editors: John Harrison and Judith Affleck

CAMBRIDGE
UNIVERSITY PRESS

CAMBRIDGE
UNIVERSITY PRESS

University Printing House, Cambridge CB2 8BS, United Kingdom

Cambridge University Press is part of the University of Cambridge.

It furthers the University's mission by disseminating knowledge in the pursuit of education, learning and research at the highest international levels of excellence.

www.cambridge.org
Information on this title: www.cambridge.org/9780521655644

© Cambridge University Press 2001

This publication is in copyright. Subject to statutory exception and to the provisions of relevant collective licensing agreements, no reproduction of any part may take place without the written permission of Cambridge University Press.

First published 2001
5th printing 2014

A catalogue record for this publication is available from the British Library

ISBN 978-0-521-65564-4 Paperback

ACKNOWLEDGEMENTS
The publisher would like to thank the following for permission to reproduce photographs: pp. 20, 54 Cambridge University Library and Greek Play Committee; p. 28 National Theatre of Greece; p. 66 The J. Paul Getty Museum, Malibu, California, attributed to Brygos Painter, Attic Red-Figure Cup Type B, Terracotta, 490–480 BC. H: 11.2 cm, Diam.: 31.4 cm, Diam. (foot): 11.2 cm; p. 80 Musée du Louvre, Paris, © Photo RMN Hervé Lewandowski; p. 86 Courtesy Museum of Fine Arts, Boston, reproduced with permission © 2000 Museum of Fine Arts, Boston, all rights reserved; p. 106 Fig A. from p. 151 of *The Cambridge Ancient History, Plates to Volumes V and VI* © Cambridge University Press.

Map on p. vii by Helen Humphreys.

Cover picture: Ajax carrying the dead Achilles, from a sixth century BC Attic vase, Museo Archeologico Nazionale, Florence.

PERFORMANCE
For permission to give a public performance of *Ajax* please write to Permissions Department, Cambridge University Press, The Edinburgh Building, Shaftesbury Road, Cambridge CB2 2RU.

Contents

Preface

The aim of the series is to enable students to approach Classical plays with confidence and understanding: to discover the play within the text.

The translations are new. Many recent versions of Greek tragedy have been done by poets and playwrights who do not work from the original Greek. The translators of this series aim to bring readers, actors and directors as close as possible to the playwrights' actual words and intentions: to create translations which are faithful to the original in content and tone; and which are speakable, with all the immediacy of modern English.

The notes are designed for students of Classical Civilisation and Drama, and indeed anyone who is interested in theatre. They address points which present difficulty to the reader of today: chiefly relating to the Greeks' religious and moral attitudes, their social and political life, and mythology.

Our hope is that students should discover the play for themselves. The conventions of the Classical theatre are discussed, but there is no thought of recommending 'authentic' performances. Different groups will find different ways of responding to each play. The best way of bringing alive an ancient play, as any other, is to explore the text practically, to stimulate thought about ways of staging the plays today. Stage directions in the text are minimal, and the notes are not prescriptive; rather, they contain questions and exercises which explore the dramatic qualities of the text. Bullet points introduce suggestions for discussion and analysis; open bullet points focus on more practical exercises.

If the series encourages students to attempt a staged production, so much the better. But the primary aim is understanding and enjoyment.

This translation of *Ajax* is based on the Oxford Classical Text edited by Hugh Lloyd-Jones and N.G. Wilson (1991). The lines of this translation follow the Greek line numbers closely.

John Harrison
Judith Affleck

Background to the story of Ajax

Ajax was a very familiar figure to the Athenians of the fifth century BC. His father was the hero Telamon, king of Salamis, and his mother was Eriboea, a princess from Athens' neighbouring state of Megara. By Sophocles' day, Salamis, the island opposite Athens' harbour, had been annexed to Athens for some time. Ajax was the eponymous hero of one of the ten tribes into which Athenians had been divided since the sixth century BC. He was therefore regarded by the people of Athens as more or less a native hero.

In Greek myth, Troy fell to Greek hands twice in consecutive generations. Ajax's father Telamon took part in the first Trojan expedition with Heracles, and distinguished himself by winning the supreme prize: Hesione, daughter of the Trojan king Laomedon. She became Telamon's captive bride, and was the mother of Ajax's half-brother **Teucer**.

Ajax took part in the second expedition to Troy led by **Agamemnon** and **Menelaus**. The story of Ajax is best known from Homer's *Iliad*, which would have been extremely familiar to Sophocles' contemporary audience. The poem is set in the tenth and final year of the Trojan war. Ajax was one of the main heroes of the poem; as a Greek warrior, he ranked second only to Achilles. His main characteristics on the battlefield were his great size and strength. He is most commonly described by Homer as 'the bulwark of the Achaeans' ('Achaeans' is Homer's preferred name for the Greek force as a whole). Ajax's captive bride, **Tecmessa**, calls him 'savage in his strength', and his son, **Eurysaces**, was named after the broad shield Ajax carried in battle. Known primarily for his reliability in a defensive role, he once almost single-handedly saved the Greek ships from being set alight and destroyed by Hector, the greatest Trojan warrior (*Iliad xii*). He also distinguished himself in combat, almost defeating Hector in a duel (*Iliad vii*). Off the battlefield, he is portrayed by Homer as straightforward and pious, a man of principle. He does not speak often, but when he does, he speaks honestly and memorably.

But the story of Ajax does not end with the *Iliad*. Homer's epic, though set in the final year of the war, ends before the actual fall of Troy. It closes with the funeral games of Patroclus – Achilles' dearest friend, killed by Hector – and the ransom and burial of Hector, whom Achilles killed to avenge Patroclus. Shortly after the events of the *Iliad*, Achilles was, in turn, killed by Paris with the help of the god Apollo. After his death, the Greek leaders, Agamemnon and Menelaus, held a contest for the supreme prize of Achilles' armour. The heroes who competed for this prize were the two men who had rescued Achilles' body from the battlefield: Ajax and **Odysseus**. Odysseus was declared the winner.

The events after the *Iliad*, up to and beyond the fall of Troy itself, are told in lost epics of the Trojan cycle, but they are also touched on retrospectively in Homer's *Odyssey*. The *Odyssey* is vague about the details of the contest for Achilles' arms. It simply states that the prize was awarded to Odysseus. The tragedian Aeschylus and the lyric poet Pindar both treated the story of Ajax before Sophocles (the relevant plays of Aeschylus are unfortunately lost). From what we know of other literature on the subject, we can pick out one or two common features of the story. Ajax seems to have been deeply dissatisfied with the way that the verdict in favour of Odysseus was reached, and he decided to take the matter into his own hands.

Sophocles' play is set in the Greek camp (most probably located to the north-west of Troy close to the open sea and the Hellespont) and takes place at some time in the period between the end of the *Iliad* and the fall of Troy, very soon after the contest for Achilles' arms and the decision against Ajax.

Map of Ancient Greece

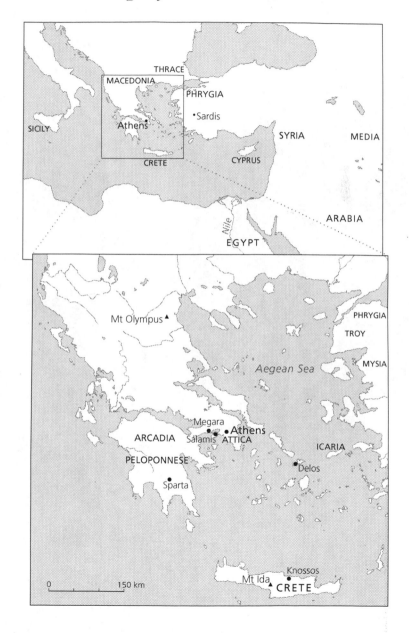

List of characters

ATHENA   *goddess of war and wisdom*

ODYSSEUS   *ruler of Ithaca, a Greek commander at Troy*

AJAX   *ruler of Salamis, a Greek commander at Troy*

CHORUS   *Ajax's men, sailors from Salamis*

TECMESSA   *Ajax's captive bride*

MESSENGER   *from the Greek army*

TEUCER   *Ajax's half-brother*

MENELAUS   *joint leader of the Greek forces at Troy, brother of Agamemnon*

AGAMEMNON   *overall leader of the Greek forces, brother of Menelaus*

PROLOGUE (1–133)

The opening scene, or prologue, generally involves a single character or a pair of characters. Sophocles favours dialogues (as seen in *Philoctetes* and *Antigone*) while Euripides prefers monologues (as seen in *Medea* and *Bacchae*).

The play is set around dawn at the Greek camp on the shore close to Troy (see map and Background to the story, pages v–vii).

Athena

Athena was the daughter of Zeus and Metis (the divine personification of intelligence). She is associated with ingenuity, warfare and handicrafts, and is particularly prominent in Homer's epics. In the *Iliad*, she fights zealously on behalf of the Greeks, assisting several heroes, including Odysseus and Achilles, but not Ajax. In the *Odyssey*, she provides constant help to Odysseus and his family.

1 Odysseus The original Greek has 'son of Laertes'.

4 edge of the line This is the most dangerous position. In the *Iliad*, the Greek forces were camped in a line along the beach with Achilles and Ajax positioned at opposite ends.

17 Etruscan trumpet A war trumpet, which may have originated in Italy, in modern-day Tuscany.

19 the shield-bearer In the *Iliad*, Ajax is often associated with his shield (see Background to the story, page v). Both here and in the *Iliad*, the size and strength of the shield reflect Ajax's own size and strength (see also 574–7).

Gods in tragedy

Gods and mortals interact regularly on the tragic stage. Occasionally the gods are fully developed characters (for example, Dionysus in Euripides' *Bacchae*). But usually, as here, they only make brief appearances. The roof of the stage building (*skēnē*) at the rear of the stage was used as an upper level for actors (see Introduction to the Greek Theatre, page 105). Unless they were major characters, gods probably appeared on top of the stage building. Characters could be lowered from this level on to the main stage, or even presented as hovering in the air, using a special crane (*mēchanē*).

Athena may be invisible to Odysseus, who describes her as **out of sight** (15). In Euripides' *Hippolytus*, Hippolytus hears but cannot see his divine patroness Artemis. But since Ajax seems to see Athena later in the scene (91), it is possible that she is visible, but out of Odysseus' view. In the ancient theatre, she may have made her first speech from above, and then been lowered by the *mēchanē* for the more intimate dialogue which follows.

AJAX

ATHENA All the time, Odysseus, I see you on the prowl,
    Hoping to seize the advantage over your enemies.
    And now I find you here beside the ships
    By Ajax's tent, where he guards the edge of the line.
    You have been stalking him for some time now,   5
    Tracing his fresh-laid tracks, to see if he is in
    Or not. Well, you have reached your goal, just like
    A keen-nosed Spartan hound. As it happens,
    He has just gone inside, his head and hands
    Dripping with sweat from his sword's deadly work.   10
    There is no need for you to peer inside those doors.
    Tell me why you have taken all this trouble,
    And learn what happened from someone who knows.
ODYSSEUS Voice of Athena, dearest of the gods! Your call
    Is so familiar, even though you are out of sight.   15
    I hear it and I take it straight to heart,
    As if it were the call of an Etruscan trumpet.
    And now, as you know, I am circling round
    For signs of my enemy, Ajax, the shield-bearer.
    He is the man I have been tracking, no one else.   20
    Last night he carried out an unimaginable crime
    Against us, if he really was the man who did it.
    We know nothing definite yet; we are still puzzled.
    That is why I volunteered to take on this task.
    We have just found our captured cattle slaughtered,   25
    Together with the men who watched the herds,
    All of them butchered at close quarters.
    Everyone is putting the blame on him.
    A watchman even saw him stride across the plain,
    All on his own with a freshly stained sword.   30
    He explained everything to me and straightaway

37 manhunt A hunting image in which Odysseus is presented as the hunter and Ajax as a victim (see also lines 1, 5–8, 31–3, 60).

● Consider the effect of Athena's use of hunting imagery in her opening speech.

41 armour of Achilles See Background to the story, page v.

Stichomythia

In tragedy there are often passages of one-line dialogue (*stichomythia*). Such passages allow the pace and emotional intensity of a scene to be varied. They also allow the relationship between two characters to be developed dynamically.

● What is the effect of *stichomythia* in a passage so early in the play (38–50, 74–88)?

53–4 beasts, not yet / Distributed Livestock captured from raids on towns near Troy was shared out among the Greek leaders.

57 Atreus' sons The sons of Atreus were Agamemnon and Menelaus, the joint leaders of the combined Greek forces.

The character of Athena

Athena seems keen to stress her own knowledge. In line 13 she describes herself as **someone who knows**. In line 36 she says, **I know, Odysseus**.

● Is this a sign of self-satisfaction, or is it simply a reminder of the omniscience which distinguishes gods from mortals?

● How does the description of Ajax's punishment in lines 51–60 affect our attitude towards a) Ajax b) Athena?

I was on his trail. Those prints I can work out,
But these are baffling; I cannot tell where he is.
You have come at the right time. From now on,
As in the past, I will let your hand guide me. 35
ATHENA I know, Odysseus. I set out some time ago,
Eager to keep an eye on your manhunt.
ODYSSEUS So, dear mistress, am I on the right track?
ATHENA Yes. This is all his doing.
ODYSSEUS But why did he lash out so senselessly? 40
ATHENA He was aggrieved about the armour of Achilles.
ODYSSEUS Then why this onslaught on our livestock?
ATHENA He meant to stain his hands with your blood.
ODYSSEUS So this attack was levelled at the Greeks?
ATHENA And it would have worked, if I had been less alert. 45
ODYSSEUS What was this plan he dared concoct?
ATHENA He set out against you alone at night, in secret.
ODYSSEUS And was he close? Did he reach his target?
ATHENA He stood at the very gates of the two leaders.
ODYSSEUS What stopped his restless hands from murder? 50
ATHENA I checked his desperate killing spree, and cast
Dark delusions over his eyes. I steered him
Towards the herds and assorted beasts, not yet
Distributed, but being watched by herdsmen.
Then he struck, hacking horned creatures to death, 55
Carving them in two, left and right. At times, he thought
He had Atreus' sons in his grasp and was killing them,
Or that he was attacking the other generals in turn.
As he ran amok in his deranged condition,
I led him on, and drove him into a cruel trap. 60

67 and tell all the Greeks One of many suggestions that Odysseus spreads rumours (see also 148–50, 187–9, 957–60).

The Homeric hero

In fifth-century Greece the heroes of the Trojan War were known primarily from Homer's *Iliad*. For Homer's heroes, cowardice was the most shameful of all vices. Cowardice was an affront to honour and reputation – the Homeric hero's primary motives for action. Athena's remark in line 75 is gauged to spur Odysseus into action.

It was customary for Homeric heroes to mock their enemies. By refusing Athena's invitation to mock Ajax (79–80), Odysseus shows that he does not share certain values typical of the Homeric hero (see also note on Ajax's sense of honour, page 34).

The character of Odysseus

In the *Iliad* and *Odyssey*, Odysseus is portrayed as resourceful and wily. While tragedians often used traditional myths and mythological figures in their plays, they felt free to reinterpret them. (A good example is Euripides' *Helen*, in which Helen is a model of virtue and never even went to Troy, but was transported by the gods to Egypt, while the Greeks and Trojans fought over a phantom likeness of her.) While Odysseus is shown in a positive light in Homer, in tragedy he is presented differently from one play to the next. In Sophocles' *Philoctetes*, for example, he is shown as manipulative and underhand in his dealings with others, whilst in *Ajax*, he is far more enlightened and honourable.

Odysseus declines Athena's invitation to mock Ajax (79–80), but he accepts her word as a goddess that Ajax will not see him (83–6).

• What picture of Odysseus emerges from these two responses to Athena?

But then, when he took a break from this work,
He tied up the cattle and sheep still left alive
And led them all back to his quarters,
As if they were men instead of horned beasts.
And now he tortures them, still tied up, in his tent.   65
I will show you his sickness, in full view,
So that you can witness it and tell all the Greeks.
Be brave! Stand your ground! Don't regard him
As a threat! I am going to distort his vision
So that he cannot see your face. You there,   70
Twisting your prisoners' arms back with ropes!
I'm calling you! Will you come out here?
I mean you, Ajax! Step outside your tent!

ODYSSEUS Athena, what are you doing? Don't call him out!

ATHENA Be quiet! Or do you want to be thought a coward?   75

ODYSSEUS Don't, for god's sake! Let him stay inside!

ATHENA In case of what? Was he not just a man before?

ODYSSEUS Yes, but he was my enemy – and still is!

ATHENA What is sweeter than laughing at your enemies?

ODYSSEUS I am happy for him to stay inside his tent.   80

ATHENA Are you scared of seeing a madman face to face?

ODYSSEUS I wouldn't be afraid if he was thinking straight.

ATHENA He won't see you now, even if you stand before him.

ODYSSEUS Why not, if he sees with the same eyes as before?

ATHENA Even though he sees, I'll darken his vision.   85

ODYSSEUS Anything is possible when a god contrives it.

88 though I would rather be anywhere else A moment of humour.
● Are there other touches of humour in the prologue?

Ajax's first appearance

As Athena tells us (81), Ajax is in a state of madness. Madness plays a key role in several tragedies (for example, the women in Euripides' *Bacchae*, and Heracles in *Hercules Furens*). It is not clear how Ajax's madness would have been presented on stage in the ancient theatre. It may have been indicated by gesture and intonation, by a special mask (see note below), or simply left to emerge from his words.
● How do Ajax's first three lines (91–3) and his replies to Athena's questions (94–110) suggest that he is not in his right mind?
○ Explore different ways of presenting Ajax's abnormal state on stage.

Masks

Actors in Greek theatre wore masks (see Introduction to the Greek Theatre, page 105). Masks may have a distancing effect upon an audience used to being able to see the actors' facial expressions.
○ Consider the advantages and disadvantages of using masks in a contemporary production.

91 child of Zeus Zeus was the king of the Olympian gods and Athena's father (see note on Athena, page 2).

92 I will crown you Precious gifts or spoils were offered as well as sacrificial animals as a mark of gratitude for divine assistance. Here, Ajax probably means that he will place offerings in a temple, or crown a statue of the goddess.

95 in the Greek army's blood Ajax believed that the animals he slaughtered were Greek soldiers (56–64). There is dramatic irony here: Athena, Odysseus and the audience all know the truth that Ajax has yet to find out.

Ajax's grievances

Ajax is angry with the whole Greek army, but with Agamemnon and Menelaus (the leaders of the Greek army) and Odysseus in particular. He believes the two leaders have insulted his honour by unfairly awarding Achilles' armour to Odysseus (see 98–100 and Background to the story, page v).
● Ajax's hatred of Agamemnon and Menelaus may seem disproportionate to their supposed offence, but winning the arms of Achilles was extremely important to Ajax. Why is this?
● Is Ajax's hatred of Odysseus understandable?

ATHENA Keep quiet, then, and stay where you are.

ODYSSEUS I'll stay, though I would rather be anywhere else.

ATHENA Ajax! This is the second time I've called you.

Why do you neglect an ally in this way?   90

AJAX Welcome, Athena! Welcome, child of Zeus!

How well you have stood by me! I will crown you

With trophies of pure gold in honour of this sport.

ATHENA Well said. But tell me this, did you

Dip your sword deep in the Greek army's blood?   95

AJAX I can make that claim; no need to deny it.

ATHENA And did you attack the sons of Atreus?

AJAX Never again will those two insult Ajax!

ATHENA They are dead, if I understand you right.

AJAX Dead. Now let them try to steal my armour!   100

ATHENA Indeed. But what about Laertes' son?

What news of him? Or has he given you the slip?

AJAX You want to know where that sly creature is?

ATHENA Yes. Where is your rival Odysseus?

AJAX He's sitting inside, a most welcome prisoner!   105

You see, I don't want him to die just yet.

ATHENA What will you do first? What more can you achieve?

AJAX First, I will tie him to a pillar in my tent...

ATHENA And what harm will you do the poor man then?

AJAX I will redden his back with my whip, then kill him.   110

ATHENA You mustn't torture the poor man like that!

117 The original text contains no stage directions, but everything suggests that at this point Ajax goes back into his tent, and that Odysseus and Athena depart at 133.

118 the power of the gods Athena is keen to emphasise the gulf between gods and mortals.
● Compare Ajax's and Odysseus' attitude to the gods.

122 'Poor man' indeed Odysseus repeats the phrase used twice by Athena in 109 and 111.
● What does Odysseus' tone, compared with that of Athena earlier, tell us about the different perspectives of mortals and gods?

Self-control
In 132–3 Athena stresses the precarious nature of human life and the gods' insistence on man's humility and self-control (*sōphrosynē*). *Sōphrosynē* is a key concept in tragedy. Tragic figures often meet with catastrophe for want of self-control, or because they do not know their place as mortals.

Staging the prologue
● How is dialogue used throughout the prologue a) to reveal information b) to create a sense of anticipation?
○ How might Athena's divine status and her special relationship with Odysseus be established on stage in a modern production (see notes on Gods in tragedy, page 2)?

PARODOS (ENTRY OF THE CHORUS) (134–200)
The Chorus (Ajax's men, sailors from Salamis) enter at 134. In the ancient theatre, they would have come on from the side entrances of the theatre and performed in the area to the front of the stage (*orchēstra*). (See Introduction to the Greek Theatre, page 105.)

The opening section of the *parodos* (134–71) is in a marching rhythm, possibly spanning the time it would have taken the Chorus to reach the *orchēstra*. They express their shame and helplessness, and show their bitterness towards Odysseus and the Greek army.

134 Telamon The father of Ajax.

135 Salamis Ajax's island home (see note on Salamis, page 44).

140 Like the eye of a winged dove Comparisons with animals are common in Greek literature.
● What ideas does this comparison suggest?

AJAX In all other things, Athena, I wish you well,
But this and nothing else will be his punishment.
ATHENA All right, if it will give you pleasure, go ahead.
Don't hold back from doing what you have planned. 115
AJAX I'll get to work. I ask only that you
Remain as strong an ally as you are now.
ATHENA You see, Odysseus, the power of the gods.
Where could you have found a more careful man,
Or one who is quicker to do what is required? 120
ODYSSEUS I know of none. He is no friend,
But still I pity him. 'Poor man' indeed –
Caught as he is in an evil delusion.
I look at myself as I look at him
And realise that all we human beings 125
Are little more than ghosts or empty shadows.
ATHENA And now that you have looked upon such things,
Never speak out against the gods yourself,
Nor swell with pride if you surpass another
In bodily strength or measure of wealth. 130
A single day can raise aloft or sink
All mortal things: the gods are fond of those
With self-control, but those without they loathe.

CHORUS   Son of Telamon, ruler of
The plains of Salamis, skirted by the sea, 135
I rejoice when you are well.
But come the stroke of Zeus,
Or raging slander from the Greeks,
I feel great alarm and fill with fear,
Like the eye of a winged dove. 140

Rumour

Rumour is an important element of the play. The first part of the play involves so much speculation because the Greeks and Ajax's friends and family (his *philoi*) are unsure of what he has done.

- What signs are there of uncertainty and curiosity on the part of the Chorus in the *parodos*?
- How do the Chorus seek to discredit the rumours about Ajax?
- Who do the Chorus mean by **men of great spirit** (154), **men of strength** (157) and **great men** (161)?
- How relevant is the argument in 154–61 to the present situation?
- Compare the two similes in lines 168 and 170 with the earlier one in the *parodos* (139–40).

Lyric passages

Besides participating in dialogue, the Chorus perform lyric passages, including the *parodos* and choral odes. Choral odes, originally set to music, are an integral part of tragedy's overall structure. They separate episodes but are closely related to the action in the dramatic sections of the play. They often comment on past action, or stimulate the audience to think about the action to come. The Chorus also danced. Along with music and singing, this was a part of the whole theatrical experience.

After the marching song, the Chorus sing a lyric ode (172–200). It takes the form of two corresponding stanzas, *strophē* (172–81) and *antistrophē* (182–91), probably sung by opposing halves of the Chorus. In the *strophē*, the Chorus speculate about which of the gods has caused Ajax's misfortune. In the *antistrophē*, they ask the gods (Zeus and Apollo in particular) to bring this misfortune to an end. The ode ends with an *epōdē* (192–200) in which the Chorus urge Ajax to help himself.

Lyric passages are centred in the text.

During the past night grievous charges
Were made against us to our shame:
They say you went across the plain
Where horses range, and destroyed
Those beasts taken by the Greeks   145
In battle but not yet handed out,
Cutting them down with your shining sword.
This is the tale Odysseus makes up
And whispers in every ear – and he wins
Men round. What he says about you now   150
Is persuasive, and those who listen
Delight in mocking your distress
More than those who tell.
One who aims at men of great spirit
Will rarely miss, but no one suggesting   155
Such things of me would be believed.
No, envy preys on men of strength,
Even though the weak make poor
Defenders of a town without them.
Small men are best supported by the great,   160
And great men best upheld by the small.
But it is impossible to teach
Judgement in these matters to fools –
And such are the men who denounce you.
Now we lack the strength, my lord,   165
To defend ourselves without you.
As long as these men escape your eye
They chatter like a flock of birds.
But if you appeared before them,
Suddenly, like a great falcon,   170
They would cower in silence, speechless.

172 Artemis Daughter of Zeus and Leto, and sister of Apollo. She was the goddess of hunting. In the original Greek she is called *Tauropola* which may mean 'protector of bulls'.

179 the War God The name in the original Greek is 'Enyalios'. It is often synonymous with Ares, the god of war.

180 some joint venture In the *Iliad*, gods and mortals often act in tandem. For example, Diomedes and Athena attacked Ares together, and Athena assisted Achilles in the killing of Hector.

Divine possession
Divine possession plays a part in many Greek myths and several tragedies. In Euripides' *Bacchae*, Dionysus, the god of ecstatic experience, possesses the women of Thebes. In Euripides' *Hippolytus*, Aphrodite, the goddess of love, causes Phaedra's fatal desire for her stepson Hippolytus.

- Since we know who is responsible for Ajax's possession, what is the effect of the Chorus' speculations in 172–81?

186 Apollo God of archery and prophecy, and the divine sender and averter of disease. In the *Iliad*, he sends a plague against the Greeks and fights on the Trojan side.

188 The supreme leaders i.e. Agamemnon and Menelaus.

189 Spawn of Sisyphus A barbed allusion to the rumour that Odysseus' mother Anticlea was with child by Sisyphus when she married his supposed father Laertes. Sisyphus was an unscrupulous trickster who, when he died, took up a famous punishment in Hades: eternally pushing a boulder up a hill so steep that he could never succeed in reaching the summit.

191 a coward's name See note on The Homeric hero, page 6.

Was it Artemis, daughter of Zeus?
What a dreadful rumour!
Origin of my disgrace!
Did *she* set you on the common herds?   175
Perhaps she was left empty-handed
After a triumph – robbed of fine war spoils
Or given nothing from a deer hunt?
Or did the War God, decked in bronze,
Feel slighted after some joint venture   180
And take revenge with a trick in the night?

Son of Telamon, you were not
In your right mind, when you went
So far astray as to fall upon the herds.
Such sickness must come from the gods.   185
I only hope Zeus and Apollo avert
This vicious rumour of the Greeks. But if
The supreme leaders or Odysseus – that cursed
Spawn of Sisyphus – spread lies in secret,
Do not hide in your tents by the shore   190
And earn yourself a coward's name.

Come, rise up from the ground where
You have been rooted for so long,
Away from battle, fanning
The flames of ruin to heaven.   195
Your enemies' insolence
Rushes on undaunted through
The airy glades, all their voices
Running wild with scathing mockery,
While I am left transfixed with pain.   200

FIRST EPISODE (201–595)

The first episode begins with dialogue between Ajax's captive wife Tecmessa and the Chorus. The metre is lyric until 263, probably to give their exchange a greater sense of urgency (it may also have been accompanied by music). The scene is still outside Ajax's tent.

Tecmessa

Tecmessa is the daughter of a Trojan noble, Teleutas. She was captured by the Greeks during a raid on a town near Troy. The Greeks had to carry out such raids throughout the Trojan war to maintain food and supplies.

Tecmessa's exact status is unclear. She is called Ajax's **captive bride** (212, 895) and she refers to herself as a slave (489, 497–9), but her relationship with Ajax, and the fact that they have a son, indicates a lasting union. The Chorus, accordingly, treat her with respect.

● What impression do we gain of Tecmessa from her opening words and the Chorus' response to her?

202 Sprung from the sons of Erechtheus Erechtheus was a mythological king of Athens. The Chorus are perhaps linked with Erechtheus to emphasise the connection between Athens and Salamis (see note on Salamis, page 44).

220 as a sacrifice Animal sacrifice was an important aspect of Greek religion. Tecmessa ironically describes Ajax's crime as a perverse sacrifice on a vast scale.

223 Unbearable yet inescapable This is one of several remarks that create an air of inevitability about Ajax's fate. With tragic figures in general, there is often a tension between this air of inevitability and a sense that catastrophe may yet be averted (see also Euripides' *Medea* and Sophocles' *Antigone*).

227 *Oi moi* Some exclamations for which there are no obvious or appropriate translations have been left in their Greek form.

TECMESSA	Crewmen of Ajax,
	Sprung from the sons of Erechtheus,
	We who care for the house of Telamon
	From far away have cause for grief.
	Now our Ajax – so huge, so fearful 205
	And savage in his strength – lies low
	Under a dark storm of sickness.
CHORUS	What grave news does this night
	Bring in place of the day's?
	Tell us, child of Phrygian Teleutas. 210
	Brave Ajax is constant in his affection
	For you, his captive bride; you should
	Be able to say from knowledge.
TECMESSA	How can I speak the unspeakable?
	The events you will hear of are as grave 215
	As death. Our famed Ajax has been put
	To shame, struck mad in the night.
	Such are the victims you can see
	In his tent, bathed in blood, slaughtered
	By his own hands as a sacrifice! 220
CHORUS	Terrible news
	About a splendid man!
	Unbearable yet inescapable!
	And loud rumour magnifies
	The story proclaimed 225
	By the leaders of the Greeks.
	Oi moi! I fear what must follow!
	He will be put to death
	In front of everyone; he whose
	Frenzied hand slaughtered the herds 230
	And their mounted herdsmen
	With a blood-red sword.

233 So it was from there, there Tecmessa now realises where the animals came from.

237–44 It is unclear whether the pair of white-hoofed rams correspond to Agamemnon and Menelaus or to one of them and Odysseus. The fact that Ajax ties the second ram to a pillar and whips it suggests that he believes it to be Odysseus (see 108–10), but the specifics of the scene are less important than the basic idea that Ajax believed the tortured animals to be his enemies.

243–4 only / A god Strange or unfamiliar occurrences were frequently attributed by the Greeks to the gods (see 185).

254 The agony of stoning Stoning was a penalty for offences against the community. In Euripides' *Bacchae*, Pentheus threatens Dionysus with stoning.

255–6 a man / Caught in a fate I could not endure There is often a strong sense of isolation about the central figure in tragedy, especially in the plays of Sophocles: compare Philoctetes, Antigone and Electra in the plays named after them. (See note on Ajax's isolation, page 34.)

The character of the Chorus
After her account of Ajax's atrocities, Tecmessa tries to impress upon the Chorus that he is now sane again. The Chorus respond pragmatically: **once trouble is over it matters less** (264). This view seems surprising after their earlier impulse to escape (245–9).
- Do such conflicting responses fit in with what we have seen of the Chorus so far?

TECMESSA   *Oi moi!* So it was from there, there
That he came with beasts in tow. Inside,
He slit the throats of some on the floor.   235
Others he carved up and tore apart.
Then, picking out two white-hoofed rams,
He severed and tossed to one side
The first one's head and the tip of its tongue.
The second he tied upright to a pillar,   240
Then, making a long horse's tether
Into a whirring double lash, he whipped it,
Letting out foul curses which only
A god could have taught him.

CHORUS   It is time to cover our heads   245
And steal away, or else
To take our places at the swift
Rowers' benches and set sail
In our seafaring ships.
Such are the threats   250
The two ruling sons of Atreus
Are plying us with!
I am terrified of sharing
The agony of stoning, and being
Struck down with him: a man   255
Caught in a fate I could not endure.

TECMESSA   Not any more. The lightning has passed.
Like a south wind that has done with raging,
He is calm once more. But being
In his right mind brings new pain.   260
To see one's own misfortune, when no one else
Is to blame, causes grave distress.

CHORUS   Still, if it has stopped, all may yet be well:
Once trouble is over it matters less.

Rational argument

A common feature of dialogue in tragedy is the use of rational argument to analyse ethical problems in the play. In 265–7 Tecmessa asks the Chorus a theoretical question which has a bearing on the present situation: would they rather be in the condition that Ajax was in before – a state of madness in which he was unaware of the distress his actions would cause – or in the condition that he is in now, where he is himself again but realises the horror of what he has done. Despite finding the argument difficult to follow at first, the Chorus agree with Tecmessa that Ajax is worse off after his return to sanity.

- How does the exchange between Tecmessa and the Chorus (257–83) affect our sympathies for Ajax?

287 I protested...

- What does Tecmessa's challenging of Ajax suggest about her character?

The Chorus from the First Cambridge Greek play, staged in 1882.

TECMESSA If given a choice, which would you prefer?   265
    To grieve your friends but feel pleasure yourself,
    Or to share the pain together with them?
CHORUS The double pain seems a greater evil.
TECMESSA So we are worse off now that he is well.
CHORUS What do you mean? I do not follow you.   270
TECMESSA When he was in the grip of sickness,
    He revelled in the evil that possessed him
    But caused us grief because we were sane.
    Now that he has found respite from his illness,
    He is overwhelmed by terrible sorrow,   275
    Yet we are no less distressed than before.
    Is that not twice the original pain?
CHORUS I agree. That is why I fear that this was a blow
    From heaven. Otherwise, why is he as unhappy,
    Now he is better, as when he was sick?   280
TECMESSA You must accept that this is how things are.
CHORUS But how did these troubles begin? Tell us
    What happened; we share your distress.
TECMESSA As it concerns you, you shall hear it all.
    At midnight, when the evening fires were dead,   285
    He took his two-edged sword and started to
    Set out, for no good reason. I protested, saying,
    'What are you doing, Ajax? Why head off
    On some venture when you haven't been summoned?
    You've heard no messengers, no trumpet-calls.   290
    Look, the whole army is now fast asleep.'

293 'Silence best becomes a woman' A version of the sentiment that 'women should be seen and not heard'. This is one of many examples of Ajax's rudeness (see 586–95) and misogyny (see 580).

Tecmessa's first major speech

Ajax's crime has been mentioned several times already (25–7, 55–6, 143–7, 229–32 and 233–44). Tecmessa, piecing together the story, now gives a broader account, including Ajax's departure from his tent and his return with the surviving animals. There seems to have been one slaughter in the place where the cattle and sheep were kept and a second in Ajax's tent. Tecmessa has first-hand knowledge of what happened in the tent, but stresses that she does not know what happened outside (see 233–4 and 295).

- How far do the events described by Tecmessa tally with what we saw in the prologue?
- How do her words make Ajax's return to sanity more vivid and painful?

303 laughing loudly Mocking enemies is part of the ethos of heroes of the *Iliad* (see note on The Homeric hero, page 6).

312 Then he threatened me with those fearful words Tecmessa clearly remembers them, but does not reveal them.

314 And asked… situation was This is one of several lines that may be interpolated (i.e. not written by Sophocles but added, possibly by actors, in later ancient productions). The reason for suspecting interpolation here is that the line is cumbersome and adds little that is of interest.

322 But like a bellowing bull Heroes in Homer's epics are often likened to powerful animals. Achilles and Ajax in the *Iliad* and Odysseus in the *Odyssey* are compared to lions. In tragedy, comparisons to powerful animals (or birds of prey) tend to suggest a heroic disposition (see the comparison of Ajax to a falcon in line 170). Bulls are particularly associated with stubbornness or implacability. In Euripides' *Medea*, Medea is said to eye her children 'like a wild bull'.

He replied bluntly with the age-old line:
'Silence best becomes a woman'.
Hearing this I gave in, and he rushed off alone.
What happened outside I cannot tell you. But he 295
Returned with his victims tied up: cattle, thick-fleeced
Sheep and the herdsmen's dogs. Some he beheaded,
Others he turned over to slit their throats or cut
Them in two, others he attacked while still tied up,
Wounding the creatures as though they were men. 300
Lastly, he sped through the doors and flung words
At shadows, first mocking the sons of Atreus,
And then Odysseus, laughing loudly
About the vengeance he had wreaked upon them.
Finally, rushing into his shelter again, 305
Somehow, slowly, with difficulty, he recovered.
And as he looked round the room full of carnage
He clapped his head and groaned. Then, sitting down,
A wreck amid the wreckage of sheep's carcasses,
He tore out his hair with his nails, fists clenched. 310
For most of the time he sat there speechless.
Then he threatened me with those fearful words
If I did not tell him all that had happened,
And asked me what his situation was.
I was afraid, my friends, and told him 315
All that he had done, as far as I knew.
And straightaway he moaned, pitiful moans
Such as I had not heard him make before.
You see, he always considered such wailing
The mark of a cowardly, low-spirited man. 320
He would groan not with high-pitched cries,
But like a bellowing bull.

324 **without food or drink** In epic and tragedy, abstinence from food and drink usually suggests inconsolability. Achilles, in the *Iliad*, rejects food and drink when grieving over the dead Patroclus. In Euripides' *Hippolytus*, Phaedra, ashamed of her lust for her stepson Hippolytus, tries to starve herself.

Offstage cries

Offstage cries are a tragic convention. The first offstage cry occurs at 333. They are usually exclamations without specific meaning, which generally convey distress (e.g. *oi moi moi* and *aiai*). They occur at times of high emotion and usually increase tension. Here, the exclamations have been left untranslated (see also note on 430).

Offstage cries occur primarily in two types of situation: during offstage violence (e.g. the murder of Medea's children in Euripides' *Medea*) and at moments of despair (e.g. the first appearance of Medea and Phaedra in Euripides' *Medea* and *Hippolytus* respectively). The usual effect is one of suspense or anticipation. Here the situation is slightly different; we have seen Ajax already. But in the prologue he was in a state of madness, whereas here he seems to be in his right mind (see 344).

● Explore the effect of Ajax's offstage cries here.

339–40 **My son, my son!** Ajax's first thought once he has returned to sanity is of his son, Eurysaces.

342 **Teucer! Where is Teucer?** Ajax next thinks of his half-brother, Teucer.

And now, laid low by such dreadful misfortune,
He sits there speechless without food or drink,
Collapsed among the butchered sheep and cattle.   325
Clearly he intends to do something drastic.
The signs are there in his words and his cries;
That is the reason I came outside, friends.
You must go in and help him if you can.
Men like him are won round by what friends say.   330

CHORUS Tecmessa, child of Teleutas, the evils
He has endured are terrible indeed.

AJAX *(offstage) Io moi moi!*

TECMESSA And it seems that things may soon be worse.
Did you not hear how Ajax cries?   335

AJAX *(offstage) Io moi moi!*

CHORUS It sounds as though he is sick, or upset
At the thought of his former sickness.

AJAX *(offstage)* My son, my son!

TECMESSA *Oi moi!* Eurysaces, he asks for you.   340
What can he want? Where are you? I am lost!

AJAX *(offstage)* Teucer! Where is Teucer? Will he go on
Endlessly raiding while I am destroyed?

CHORUS He seems to have regained his sanity. Open the doors!
Seeing me may restore his sense of shame.   345

TECMESSA All right, I'll open them. See for yourself
What he has done and what condition he is in.

Ajax's second appearance

The section 348–429 is a lyric passage arranged in three corresponding pairs of stanzas, each with *strophē* and *antistrophē* (348–55 and 356–63; 364–78 and 379–93; 394–411 and 412–29).

In the classical theatre, Ajax would probably have been wheeled on stage through the central stage doors at 348 on a round platform called the *ekkyklēma*, which was used specifically to show interior scenes. Here it would represent the inside of Ajax's tent (stage props would possibly be used to create this effect).

- What do Ajax's initial words (348–53 and 356–61) tell us about his state of mind? What is the effect of the sea imagery here, and why is it appropriate to the Chorus? (See page 10, The entry of the Chorus.)
- How might a similar effect be produced on the modern stage?

Violence

As a rule, violence was not shown on stage in tragedy. In Euripides' *Medea*, the murder of her children is heard offstage but not shown. In Euripides' *Bacchae*, the death of Pentheus is made more shocking by the appearance of his mother Agave with his decapitated head. Here, the after-effects of Ajax's crime are shown to convey the horror of what he did.

361 Come, kill me with these beasts! Tragic characters often express a desire for death. In Euripides' *Medea*, despite her grim triumph by the end of the play, Medea initially expresses a wish to die.

- We are used to background music in film and television, but how might musical accompaniment be used to enhance the impact of lyric passages in modern performances of tragedy?

Ajax's character

Ajax pays little attention to Tecmessa or the Chorus. He does not even mention the slaughter of the herdsmen (see 26). Instead, he dwells on the mockery of his enemies (see 367 and 382).

- What do we learn about him from his perception of his misfortune? Does he show any signs of remorse?
- How sympathetic a character is Ajax a) before his appearance at 348 b) by the end of the second *antistrophē* at 393?

AJAX   *Io!*
                    Dear sailors, my only friends,
                        You alone remain true.   350
                    Do you see the wave, raised
                    By a deadly storm, which swirls
                    Around me and engulfs me?

CHORUS *Oi moi*, it seems that your account was all too true.
        This plainly shows he is not himself.   355

AJAX   *Io!*
                    Men skilled in the art of sailing,
                        Who ply your oars at sea,
                    You, you are the only ones
                        I see to take care of me.   360
                    Come, kill me with these beasts!

CHORUS Watch your words! Don't try to cure wrong with wrong,
        And make your pain worse than your plight.

AJAX   See how bold I was, how brave of heart,
                    And fearless before my enemies –   365
                    Laying grim hands on docile beasts!
                Oi moi! How laughable! How humiliating!

TECMESSA Lord Ajax, I beg you, don't talk like that!
AJAX Get out of here! Go back outside!
        Aiai aiai!   370
TECMESSA I implore you, listen and show some sense!

387 Zeus, father of my forefathers Ajax's paternal grandfather
Aeacus (also grandfather to Achilles) was the son of Zeus.

392 When you pray for this, ask that I should die too Compare
Tecmessa's exclamation with Ajax's wish to die in 387–91.
- Does Tecmessa actually want to die or is she trying to elicit some
  kind of response from Ajax?

398–400 I am no longer fit / To look to gods for help
- Why does Ajax see himself as unworthy of being helped? How does
  this statement relate to his appeal at 387–91?

*Ajax, Tecmessa and Eurysaces in a production by the Greek National
Theatre, 1961.*

AJAX   How wretched I am, to let
                     Those fiends slip through my hands,
                     And attack horned cattle
                     And fine sheep, spilling   375
                     Their dark blood instead!

CHORUS Why grieve over what is already done?
        These things could not be otherwise.

AJAX   You who see and hear all things,
                     The instrument of every crime,   380
                Son of Laertes, foulest creature in the army,
                You must be laughing out loud with joy.

CHORUS It is in the lap of the gods, who laughs and cries.
AJAX Still, I would like to find him, ruined as I am.
      Io moi moi!   385
CHORUS No proud words! Look at the state you are in!

AJAX   Zeus, father of my forefathers,
                     If only I could destroy that
                     Arch-deceiver, hateful creature,
                     And those two brother kings,   390
                     And then, finally, die myself!

TECMESSA When you pray for this, ask that I should die too.
          What have I to live for once you are gone?

AJAX   *Io!* Darkness, my sole light!
                     Death's shadows, so clear to me!   395
                     Take me! Take me
                     To live with you!
                     I am no longer fit
                     To look to gods for help,
                     No, nor mortals neither.   400

401 The daughter of Zeus Ajax suddenly seems to realise that Athena is responsible for his downfall. It is strange that no explanation is given of how he acquires this understanding (see also 449–53).

Ajax's despair

In 394–5 Ajax expresses his despair by reversing the customary association of light with life and hope and darkness with death and despair.

- How is Ajax's sense of isolation brought out at 394–409?
- What is the tone of Ajax's words at 412–27? What signs are there of a) resignation b) defiance?

418 O streams of Scamander Scamander (also known as Xanthus) is one of the two rivers near Troy. The other is called Simoïs.

421–5 a man... / Like no other that Troy / Has set eyes on, of all / The men who came from Greece In the *Iliad*, Ajax is the second best Greek warrior, the supremacy of Achilles being beyond question.

- Is Ajax's claim here excessive or is he somehow asserting his uniqueness without challenging Achilles' supremacy?

426–7 Even though now I lie here / Like this, deprived of honour This indignation at the failure of the Greek leaders to recognise his worth is something Ajax shares with Achilles. In the *Iliad*, Achilles felt that Agamemnon had dishonoured him by taking away his prize, a girl named Briseis. Here, Ajax believes that Agamemnon and the other Greeks have dishonoured him by awarding Achilles' armour to Odysseus.

The daughter of Zeus,
That powerful goddess,
Torments me to death.
Where can I escape? Where can I
Take refuge? My great deeds are all
Wiped out, along with these beasts.
The hunt I went on was mindless,
And now the whole army will surely
Take up their swords and cut me down!

TECMESSA Ah me, that a fine man should voice such thoughts; 410
Words that he never would have said before.

AJAX

Io! Paths of the pounding sea!
Coastal caves and groves of the shore!
For a long, long time you have kept me
Here at Troy. But no longer! 415
Let all men of reason know
That I will breathe this air no more!
O streams of Scamander,
That flow alongside us, so bitter
To the Greeks, no more will you 420
Look upon a man – now I
Shall make my grand claim –
Like no other that Troy
Has set eyes on, of all
The men who came from Greece, 425
Even though now I lie here
Like this, deprived of honour.

CHORUS I cannot stop you, but I can't let you go on,
When you have suffered such grievous misfortune.

Ajax's first major speech (430–80)

Apart from his appearance in the prologue, Ajax has so far only spoken in emotionally intense lyric outbursts. His first major speech is no less intense, but it is in the customary metre for monologues and dialogues. In this speech, Ajax offers a more reasoned, coherent description of his plight.

430 *Aiai!* Ajax draws attention to the fact that his name is similar to this cry of sorrow (the Greek spelling of Ajax's name is *Aias*). Etymological interpretations of names are common in tragedy; Ajax's name means something like 'man of sorrow'. In Euripides' *Bacchae*, Pentheus' name is related to the word *penthos*, meaning 'grief'.

434 this land of Ida Ida is a mountain near Troy.

Telamon

Ajax's father is mentioned several times by Ajax and later by his half-brother Teucer (1299–1303). In 434–6 Ajax describes his father's achievements in a previous expedition to Troy with Heracles. Telamon won Teucer's mother Hesione, King Laomedon's daughter, as a special prize.

- What comparable prize has Ajax won?
- How does the looming presence of Telamon affect our attitude towards Ajax?

454 They mock me now Ajax again focuses on the mockery of others as something intolerable (see note on Ajax's sense of honour, page 34).

AJAX *Aiai!* Who ever would have thought that my name 430
 Would chime so well with my condition!
 Time for me to cry '*aiai*' again,
 And a third time, so deep are my troubles.
 My father went home from this land of Ida
 After winning the army's highest honours, 435
 And brought back with him all manner of glory.
 Now I have come to this same land of Troy,
 His son, in no way his inferior in strength –
 My hands have performed deeds no less
 Than his – yet I am ruined like this, dishonoured 440
 By the Greeks. Even so, I think I know
 This much: if Achilles were alive to award
 The crown for valour in a contest for his arms,
 No one else would receive them before me.
 But the sons of Atreus made the prize over to 445
 An evil-minded man, ignoring my achievements.
 And if my eyes and this warped mind had not
 Swerved from my purpose, they would not have lived
 To judge another as they did me. As it was,
 Zeus' invincible daughter, goddess of the stern eyes, 450
 Deceived me with a plague of madness
 Just as I was raising my hands against them,
 So that I stained my palms with these beasts' blood.
 They mock me now, the men who have escaped me –
 No wish of mine – but if a god steps in, 455
 Even a coward may escape his betters.
 And what should I do now? I am loathed by the gods
 (That much is clear), the Greek army hates me,
 Even Troy and its surrounding plains detest me!

461 over the Aegean The Aegean is the sea between the eastern coast of Greece and Asia Minor (modern-day Turkey). See map on page vii.

Ajax's isolation

Tragic heroes and heroines are often marked by a sense of isolation (see also note on 255–6). In Euripides' *Medea*, Medea feels alone not only because she is foreign and female, but because she is banished by King Creon and forsaken by her husband. Ajax is equally isolated. He is absent from the battlefield (see 190–1) and wonders whether to stay at Troy or go home (457–65). But either of these options would have dire consequences: if he goes home it will be in disgrace and if he stays he will probably face a humiliating death.

- Ajax considers a third option: storming the citadel alone (466–8). How rational a plan does this seem? What does his rejection of this idea tell us about his motives?
- How does Sophocles create a progressive sense of isolation and desperation in Ajax's train of thought throughout this speech?

Ajax's sense of honour

The tragic Ajax of this play shares a number of qualities with Ajax as depicted in the *Iliad* and other Homeric heroes such as Achilles and Hector (see note on The Homeric hero, page 6). Heroes in this mould are emotionally intense, inflexible and strong-willed, intolerant of injustice and mockery, and they characteristically exhibit a fierce sense of honour and a 'death or glory' attitude to life.

In lines 475–6, Ajax expresses the idea that life without honour is worthless. Achilles adopts a similar stance in *Iliad* ix when he refuses a vast reward, offered to him by Agamemnon as compensation for having dishonourably confiscated his prize, on the grounds that thereby his honour would still not be restored properly. Honour is the essential compensation for a short life involving many risks. Ajax states at 479–80 that one may live long provided that one lives greatly, otherwise one must die greatly. There is, perhaps, an implication that Ajax is going to follow this rule through himself.

Should I desert the sons of Atreus, leave this haven 460
For ships, and go back over the Aegean? But how
Could I show my face to my father Telamon?
How could he bring himself to look at me
Returning empty-handed with no victory prize,
When he himself brought home the crown of glory? 465
It is unthinkable. Perhaps I could
Storm Troy's walls, one against them all, perform
Some great feat and then, finally, be killed?
But that way I might please the sons of Atreus,
And that cannot be. No, I have to find 470
A way of proving to my aged father that,
At least by nature, his son is no coward.
It is shameful for a man to crave long life,
If he is never released from misfortune.
What joy is there in being flung towards death 475
And then snatched back again day after day?
I rate as worthless any human being
Who kindles his spirit on empty hopes.
A truly noble man must live with honour
Or die with honour. That is all I have to say. 480
CHORUS Ajax, no one would say your words
Are false; you clearly spoke your mind.
All the same, you must stop and put aside
These thoughts. Let your will be guided by friends.

488 Phrygia An area just to the east of Troy (see map on page vii).

Tecmessa's second major speech (485–524)

Tecmessa's speech tells us more about her character and forms a closely argued response to Ajax's speech. She begins by mentioning her good birth (487–8, see note on Tecmessa, page 16), but stresses her acceptance of misfortune (488–90). Her use of the word 'slave' perhaps implies that she can genuinely sympathise with Ajax's reversal of fortune *(peripateia)* now.

● How personal is Tecmessa's speech and to what extent does this help to evoke our sympathy?
● Is her plea made more pitiful by her use of the word 'concubine' instead of 'wife' in line 50?

Throughout her speech Tecmessa acknowledges Ajax's heroic nature while underlining her complete dependence on him. After an entreaty on behalf of Ajax's parents, Tecmessa asks him to think of their son, and, finally, of her. In her final bid for sympathy (514–24), she emphasises her own helplessness and appeals to Ajax's sense of honour.

● How persuasive is her final appeal?

Homeric echoes

Tecmessa's description of being mocked by a new Greek master (501–3) closely echoes part of a memorable scene in *Iliad vi* between Hector, eldest son of King Priam, and his wife Andromache. In her attempt to dissuade Hector from fighting Achilles, Andromache imagines her fate if he is killed and Troy falls. In this context, what Tecmessa imagines in 501–3 is a striking reflection of the enmity that has now arisen between Ajax and his fellow Greeks.

In 510–13 Tecmessa hopes that Ajax will be moved by paternal concern (see note on 339–40). The lines again echo the scene between Andromache and Hector in the *Iliad* where Andromache asks Hector to think of their son Astyanax's future.

516–17 The cause of the death of Tecmessa's parents is left unclear.

TECMESSA My lord Ajax, there is no greater evil   485
    For mankind than the grip of fate.
    I was born the child of a free man,
    As wealthy as anyone in Phrygia. But now
    I am a slave: so the gods and, most of all,
    Your own right hand decreed. But since I share   490
    Your bed and care for you, I beg you now,
    By Zeus who guards the hearth, and by the bed
    In which we were united, do not allow me
    To suffer the painful jibes of your enemies
    By leaving me as a captive to one of them.   495
    If you die, and by your death forsake me,
    Know that on that very day I will be taken
    Forcibly, together with your son, by the Greeks
    And made to lead a life of servitude.
    Then some lord will mock me with bitter insults,   500
    Words like these: 'Look, the concubine of Ajax,
    Who used to be the strongest in the army.
    How menial her tasks, whose life was once envied!'
    So he will say, and I shall bear my lot,
    And his words will shame you and all your kin.   505
    Think of your father, abandoning him
    In grim old age, and your mother as well,
    Blessed with long life. How often she has prayed
    To the gods for you to return home safely.
    And pity your son, my lord, if he must be raised   510
    Without you, deprived of the care a young child needs,
    With loveless foster parents. Think how much
    Harm you will cause him and me if you die.
    I have nothing to look to except you.
    You destroyed my homeland with your spear,   515
    While another fate dispatched my mother and father
    To dwell below in Hades among the dead.

Ajax's reaction

After Tecmessa's speech the Chorus urge Ajax to show Tecmessa pity. There then follows a short section of *stichomythic* dialogue between Tecmessa and Ajax (see note on *Stichomythia*, page 4).

● Compare Ajax's reaction to Tecmessa's speech with her attitude towards Ajax. How is their dialogue used to explore the relationship between Ajax and Tecmessa?

542 Bring him here, whoever is leading him! This suggests that Ajax's son may be as young as three or four. At any rate, given that the war has been going for a little under ten years, he could be no more than nine.

What country can I call my own without you?
What wealth have I? My entire welfare hinges
On you. Spare a thought for me. A man should   520
Remember where he has found happiness.
Kindness begets kindness, and any man
Who lets his blessings slip his mind
Should no longer be regarded as noble.

CHORUS Ajax, I hope you can find pity in your heart,   525
As I have. Then you would approve her words.

AJAX She will indeed win my approval, so long as
She means to carry out my orders properly.

TECMESSA Beloved Ajax, I will obey you in everything.

AJAX Then bring my son here, so that I can see him.   530

TECMESSA I had him removed out of fear.

AJAX Because of all this trouble? Is that what you mean?

TECMESSA The poor boy might have met you and been killed.

AJAX That would have been in keeping with my luck!

TECMESSA At least I made sure of preventing that.   535

AJAX I approve your action, and your presence of mind.

TECMESSA Given how things stand, how can I be of help?

AJAX Let me talk to the boy and see him face to face.

TECMESSA Of course, servants are looking after him nearby.

AJAX What's the delay? Why is he not here yet?   540

TECMESSA My child, your father's calling you!
    Bring him here, whoever is leading him!

Ajax's second major speech

Ajax's second long speech is addressed to his son Eurysaces. The speech, like Tecmessa's (lines 485–524), recalls the scene in the *Iliad* with Hector, Andromache and their son Astyanax (see note on Homeric echoes, page 36). The speech also introduces Ajax's half-brother Teucer as a key figure in the play.

- To what extent does the speech emphasise Ajax's harshness and self-centredness? Is there any evidence of a humane or tender side to his character?
- How effectively does Ajax respond to the specific aspects of Tecmessa's appeal (see especially 506–13 and 520–4)?

Children on stage

Children appear occasionally on the tragic stage, but their parts are non-speaking insofar as they are not given whole lines. Eurysaces' part is silent, but in Euripides' *Medea*, the children, who are a focal point throughout the play, utter piteous cries when they are murdered by their mother offstage.

545 Lift him up, lift him up here! This suggests that Ajax is raised off the ground, probably on a heap of carcasses.

546 the sight of all this freshly / Spilt blood Ajax's stern remark contrasts with the atmosphere in the scene with Hector and Andromache in *Iliad vi*. When Hector's son Astyanax flinches at the sight of the crest on his father's helmet, his amused parents comfort him, and the whole scene is a fleeting tableau of domestic harmony. At 558–9, there is a rare moment when Ajax shows similar tenderness towards his wife and child.

548 broken in straight away The image of taming horses is a suitably martial metaphor for Ajax.

556–7 you must show / Your enemies Ajax simply cannot overlook the disrespect shown to him by Agamemnon and Menelaus.

571 the dark realm of the god below The god below is Hades, god of the underworld.

572 At this point, Ajax reverts suddenly to the subject of arms. What tenderness there was in his remarks about his son and wife (558–9) and his parents (568–71) now disappears.

AJAX Is he coming? Did he hear you?

TECMESSA The servant is bringing him in right now.

AJAX Lift him up, lift him up here! He will not   545
Be frightened by the sight of all this freshly
Spilt blood, not if he is my true-born son.
He needs to be broken in straight away,
His nature shaped to his father's harsh ways.
Son, may you be luckier than your father,   550
But like him in all else; then you will be no coward.
Yet even now I envy you one thing:
You have no idea of these troubles.
Life without understanding is most sweet,
Before you come to learn of grief or joy.   555
When you reach that stage you must show
Your enemies what kind of father's son you are.
But in the meantime feed on gentle breezes,
Nurse your tender soul, as your mother's joy.
I know that none of the Greeks will abuse you   560
With spiteful insults, even if you are without me.
I shall leave you Teucer as a staunch guardian.
He will look after you faithfully, even though
He is far off now hunting enemies. But you,
My armoured warriors, seafaring men,   565
I entrust you with this collective favour,
And make sure you express my will to Teucer:
Escort this boy back to my house and show him
To Telamon and my mother, Eriboea, so that
He may bring them comfort in their old age,   570
Until they reach the dark realm of the god below.
And let no judges, nor the man who ruined me,
Set up my arms as a prize for the Greeks.

574–7 Ajax's son takes his name from his father's distinctive, broad shield, which is described at 574–7 and also in the *Iliad* as seven-layered and impregnable. In the prologue Odysseus refers to him as **the shield-bearer** (see note on 19).

The end of Ajax's speech

- Is there a shift of tone towards the end of Ajax's speech? To what might this be attributed?
- Consider the tone of the last two lines in particular. What is the effect of this final image?

584 I do not like the sharp edge of your voice The Chorus pick up on the image presented by Ajax in 581–2.

586 Show self-control!

- Who is most lacking in self-control: Ajax or Tecmessa?

591–4 In this section Ajax and Tecmessa speak in alternate half-lines. This increases the emotional tempo and intensity to an even greater extent than *stichomythia* (see note on page 4).

594–5 You must be a fool / If you think you can change my nature now After displaying stubbornness, Ajax shows his awareness of this aspect of his character. Self-conscious stubbornness is a characteristic found in several tragic heroes and heroines (for example Medea in Euripides' *Medea* and Antigone and Creon in Sophocles' *Antigone*).

- How does Ajax's attitude to the gods in 586–95 compare with what we have seen of him in the play so far (see lines 112–13, 398–9, 401–5, 449–58)?

Staging the scene

It is unclear what would have happened on the ancient stage at the end of this dialogue. Eurysaces may have been taken offstage by an attendant between 578 and 582. Alternatively, Tecmessa may have taken charge of him. Ajax was probably wheeled offstage on the *ekkyklēma* (see note on Ajax's second appearance, page 26), but Tecmessa (and Eurysaces, if he remained with his mother) may well have stayed on stage during the choral ode which follows, since she is on stage with the Chorus for Ajax's speech after the ode (see 685).

Eurysaces, my son, hold this from which
You take your name: my seven-layered,   575
Impregnable shield. Carry it holding it by
The well-stitched handle. My other arms shall be
Buried with me. Now take my son, quickly,
And close the door! Don't cry in front of the tent!
Women are all too fond of tears!   580
Shut it! Quick! A good surgeon chants no hymns
For a condition that warrants the knife!
CHORUS I fear this urgency of yours, and
I do not like the sharp edge of your voice.
TECMESSA Lord Ajax, what are you planning to do?   585
AJAX Don't judge or question me. Show self-control!
TECMESSA *Oi moi*, I despair! By your son
And by the gods, I beg you: don't betray us!
AJAX You plague me too much! You must know
That I no longer owe the gods anything!   590
TECMESSA Watch your words!
AJAX   Tell someone who'll listen!
TECMESSA Won't you listen?
AJAX   You've said too much already!
TECMESSA I'm afraid, my lord.
AJAX   Shut the door, quickly!
TECMESSA Relent, I beg you!
AJAX   You must be a fool
If you think you can change my nature now.   595

Salamis

Salamis, the island home of Ajax and the Chorus, lies opposite Piraeus, the main harbour of Athens. It was annexed to Athens in the sixth century BC. The whole of the following ode is addressed to the island.

FIRST CHORAL ODE (1ST *STASIMON*) (596–645)

This kind of choral ode or lyric interlude, which both links and punctuates the episodes that precede and follow it, is called a *stasimon*. The mood of the ode is sombre. In the *strophē* of the first pair of stanzas (596–608) the Chorus express their nostalgia and dejection. In the *antistrophē* (609–21) they lament Ajax's present condition. In the second pair of stanzas (622–33 and 634–45) they pity Ajax's mother and father and conclude, pessimistically, that their son would be better off dead.

- How does the Chorus' nostalgia compare with Ajax's perception of home in 460–6?
- How does the Chorus' response to the prospect of dying (600–608) compare with Ajax's attitude to death (see 387–409, 470–80 and 545–82)?

600 But I have suffered long The play is set shortly after the end of the *Iliad*, in the tenth and final year of the Trojan war.

608 Hades, the grim destroyer This view of Hades, the god of the Underworld, may be compared to the medieval image of the 'grim reaper'. Hades, however, is a much broader concept which signifies the Underworld itself as well as its presiding deity.

613 you put him forth Here, **you** refers to Salamis.

615–21 This description of Ajax is reminiscent of several descriptions of Achilles' isolation in the *Iliad*, in which he spends long periods of time thinking alone in his tent or on the beach.

CHORUS   Glorious Salamis,
You sit happily,
Lapped by waves,
Ever conspicuous to all.
But I have suffered long,   600
Encamped here upon
The grassy plains
Beneath Mount Ida,
Waiting countless months,
Worn by the march of time,   605
With only the bleak prospect,
One day, of reaching
Hades, the grim destroyer.

Alongside me is Ajax,
A man past curing,   610
Stricken with madness
Sent by the gods.
In the past you put him forth,
A powerful man in the heat of battle.
Now he nurses his thoughts alone,   615
A source of great sorrow to friends.
The exploits of his hands,
The greatest achievements,
Are gone, gone, having earned
No love from the wretched,   620
Loveless sons of Atreus.

628–9 melancholy laments / Like those of the forlorn nightingale
In myth, the nightingale was originally a woman called Procne. Her
husband Tereus raped her sister Philomela and cut off her tongue so
that she could never tell of the crime. But Philomela made a tapestry
depicting her torment and managed to send it to Procne, who then
killed her own son and served him up to Tereus as a meal by way of
revenge. Procne, Philomela and Tereus were all turned into birds –
nightingale, swallow and hoopoe respectively – and the nightingale's
song was believed to be Procne's lament for her lost son. The story of
Tereus, Philomela and Procne was the subject of Sophocles' last play
Tereus.

631–3 blows from her fists Pounding one's chest and tearing out
one's hair are the customary form of grieving in the *Iliad*. At the death
of Hector, Priam even covered himself in dung.

**636–8 A man who by birth was among / The noblest of the long-
suffering / Achaeans** Ajax, like Achilles, also belonged to the house of
Aeacus (see note on The house of Atreus, page 92). Achaea is a specific
region of Greece but is being used here to refer to Greece as a whole.
In the *Iliad*, too, the Greeks are known as Achaeans.
● How has the mood of the play altered during the choral ode?

Staging the ode
In an ancient production, if Tecmessa remained on stage after the
doors to Ajax's tent were closed (see notes on Staging the scene, page
42), it is unclear whether or not she would have acknowledged the
Chorus' words.
● How might Tecmessa's presence or absence affect the impact of this
ode?

Surely his mother, who has
Lived through so many years,
White with old age,
Hearing that he has been struck   625
With sickness of the mind,
Will not hold back, poor woman,
From melancholy laments
Like those of the forlorn nightingale;
No, she will cry out the shrill   630
Notes of a dirge, blows from her fists
Will pound her breast, and her
White hair will be torn.

Better for one who is sick
Beyond hope to lie in Hades.   635
A man who by birth was among
The noblest of the long-suffering
Achaeans no longer behaves
As he used to,
But acts out of character.   640
Poor father, you have yet to learn
The nature of your son's
Unbearable curse, which no other
Member of the house of Aeacus
Has suffered except him.   645

SECOND EPISODE (646–92)

This episode is brief but momentous. Ajax comes out of his tent to deliver a long speech, after which he departs alone.

Ajax's third major speech (646–92)

Ajax begins (646–8) by stressing the power of time to bring about change (a similar idea has already been expressed from a different perspective by Athena in lines 131–2 of the prologue). This partly explains Ajax's own change from implacability to compliance (648–52). The other reason for the change, says Ajax, is his pity for Tecmessa. Implying that he no longer wishes to die, he resolves to purify himself, dispose of his sword, and submit to Agamemnon and Menelaus.

654–5 I will go to the pools Ritual washing was a way of ridding oneself of the guilt of a crime involving the unlawful spilling of blood.

656 The grievous anger of the goddess i.e. Athena (see note on 401).

662–5 a gift from Hector In *Iliad iv*, after an inconclusive duel between Menelaus, the rightful husband of Helen, and Paris, her abductor and lover, there followed an intense period of fighting. After this, in *Iliad vii*, the two sides agreed to another duel. The Greeks drew lots to fight Hector, the greatest Trojan warrior, and Ajax was chosen. The duel was stopped and declared a draw, even though Ajax seemed to have the upper hand, and as a mark of mutual respect the two men exchanged gifts: Hector gave Ajax his sword and Ajax gave Hector his war belt.

666–8 From now on I shall give in to the gods / And learn to submit

- Compare these lines with Ajax's previous attitude to Agamemnon and Menelaus (see 97–100, 387–91). How plausible does this change of heart seem?

AJAX The long and countless lapse of Time brings forth
All things from darkness and then hides them from
The light. Nothing is past belief; the stubborn will
Or solemn promise can be overturned.
Why, even I, who seemed till now so hard,   650
As iron is when dipped, have been made soft
By this woman's words. For pity I cannot leave
A widow and an orphan to my enemies.
No, I will go to the pools in the groves
By the shore to cleanse my guilt and escape   655
The grievous anger of the goddess. After that,
I shall go and find some untrodden place
To bury my sword – most hateful of weapons –
And hide it in the earth where none will see it.
Let the darkness of Hades keep it there below!   660
From the moment my hands received it
As a gift from Hector, worst of my enemies,
I have suffered only ill from the Greeks.
And so it seems that the proverb is true:
The gift of an enemy brings no good at all.   665
From now on I shall give in to the gods
And learn to submit to the sons of Atreus.
As leaders they must be followed, no question.
Even the greatest and most awesome forces
Bow to authority: so winter's snows   670
Retreat before the fruitfulness of summer;
So night in its endless cycle retires
For day with her white steeds to kindle light;
And so the blast of fierce winds stills
The murmuring sea. Even all-conquering sleep   675
Cannot bind for ever, but must relax its grip.
How, then, can we refuse to know our place?

686 as my heart desires Though his most frequent wish has been for death, his most recent was to appease Athena (654–6).

689 he must tend to my needs and support you Teucer would only have to support Tecmessa if Ajax were not there to do so himself.
- Does this suggest anything about Ajax's intentions?

The intention of Ajax's third speech
The speech has provoked a great deal of argument about whether Ajax is being sincere, deceitful, or truthful in a way calculated to mislead.
- Which lines are ambiguous? Do the language and structure of the speech provide any answers?
- If Ajax is misleading the others, does this in itself undermine the value of the beliefs that he sets forth?
- How does the speech affect our impression of Ajax's character?
Whatever his intentions, the speech allows him to leave the stage unimpeded, and to be alone to act while the others are off their guard.

SECOND CHORAL ODE (2ND *STASIMON*) (693–718)
The second choral ode is a short song of jubilation consisting of a corresponding *strophē* (693–705) and *antistrophē* (706–18). The Chorus express relief and delight. They thank Pan and Apollo (gods linked with dance and music), and hail Ajax's supposed recovery.
- Compare the tone of this ode with the first *stasimon* (596–645). What is the effect of the Chorus' uninhibited joy at this point?

692 Tecmessa probably leaves the stage at this point (see notes on line 784–5 and Staging the scene, page 42).

696 Cyllene A mountain in Arcadia, where Pan lived (see map on page vii).

699 The Cretan and Mysian steps Crete and Mysia are places whose names are associated with dances (see map on page vii).

702 Lord of Delos Apollo was born on, and strongly associated with, the holy island of Delos (see map).

704 Icarian waters Icaria is an island in the Aegean (see map).

I, for one, do. I have come to learn lately
That we should only hate our enemies
As men who may in future become friends.   680
And I intend to help friends as if they may not
Always remain so; for most of mankind
The harbour of friendship is treacherous.
But all these things will turn out well. So you
Go inside, woman, and pray to the gods   685
That all will transpire as my heart desires.
And you, my friends, respect my wishes
As she does, and tell Teucer, when he comes,
That he must tend to my needs and support you.
I shall be going to the place I must.   690
But you do as I say and, though I suffer now,
You should hear very soon that all is well.

CHORUS   I thrill with longing and leap
                With delight. O Pan, Pan, roaming
                    The sea, appear to us from   695
                Cyllene's jagged, snow-capped ridge.
                    Lord of the dances of gods,
                Appear, that you may tread with me
                    The Cretan and Mysian steps
                    That you have taught yourself!   700
                    Now is the time for dancing!
                    May Apollo, Lord of Delos,
                    Make his way, visible across
                The Icarian waters, and join me,
                    Remaining forever kindly.   705

706 Ares has banished sore grief Ares was the god of war. Perhaps the Chorus see Ares as the source of Ajax's troubles – after all, his problems started over a contest for arms (see also 179–81).

714–15 Great Time makes all things fade; / I would say nothing is beyond belief

- The Chorus' words closely paraphrase Ajax's in 646–8.

THIRD EPISODE (719–814)
Just when the characters closest to Ajax begin to feel more confident of his recovery, a messenger arrives with disturbing news.

Messenger speeches
Speeches by minor characters – messengers, servants or shepherds – to relate offstage events are a common feature in Greek tragedy. Some plays, such as Sophocles' *Oedipus Tyrannus*, have more than one such speech.

Messenger speeches are usually emotionally charged pieces of narrative, whose technique and style are comparable to that of epic poetry, particularly in their use of direct speech and vivid detail. The speeches offer a great deal of scope for an actor to bring them to life.

Offstage events may be narrated for two main reasons: because they are too violent or complex to present on stage (e.g. Medea's murder of Creon's daughter in Euripides' *Medea* and the dismemberment of Pentheus in Euripides' *Bacchae*), or because they take place elsewhere or prior to the action of the play.

Teucer's arrival in the Greek camp, though nearby, takes place elsewhere, and is slightly prior to the current action. The threatening of Teucer by the whole Greek army would have been hard to show on stage because of the numbers required. Narrating Teucer's arrival before his appearance on stage also creates a sense of anticipation.

720 the hills of Mysia Mysia is part of north-west Turkey. The Mysians were Trojan allies.

726 the kinsman of 'that maniac…' The word **kinsman** may be used as a jibe, as Teucer was only the half-brother of Ajax.

Ares has banished sore grief
From our eyes. *Io io!*
Now, once again, O Zeus,
Can sparkling daylight shine
Upon our swift sea-going ships.   710
Ajax is once again free of pain,
And has fulfilled the laws of the gods
With due rites, observing strictest piety.
Great Time makes all things fade;
I would say nothing is beyond belief   715
When, against all expectation,
Ajax has laid aside his anger towards
The sons of Atreus and his great quarrel!

MESSENGER My friends, I wish to tell you first that Teucer
Has just returned from the hills of Mysia.   720
But as he headed for the camp headquarters,
He was reviled by all the Greeks in unison.
Sensing his arrival from some way off,
They flocked round and drubbed him with insults
From all directions, every one of them.   725
They branded him the kinsman of 'that maniac
Who betrayed the army', and said they would not rest
Until he was dashed to pieces by stones.
Things even reached the point where swords
Were drawn and at the ready.   730
But when the confrontation came to a head,
The words of the elders restored the peace.
But where is Ajax? I must speak to him –
Tell all the news to those whom it concerns.

Calchas

Prophets are important figures in Greek myth. The two best-known prophets in Classical literature are Calchas and Tiresias, who appear in the *Iliad* and *Odyssey* respectively. Tiresias appears in several tragedies (including Euripides' *Bacchae* and Sophocles' *Oedipus* and *Antigone*). Both Calchas and Tiresias give important, and infallible, indications of what is to come in the play as well as insight into the will of the gods. Prophets generally help to create dramatic tension and suspense, as their advice is usually ignored (by Oedipus in *Oedipus* and Pentheus in *Bacchae*) or heeded too late (by Creon in *Antigone*). Here it is implied, rather than stated, that Calchas is infallible (745–6, 782–3). He is also shown as being well-disposed to Ajax (751), despite his criticisms of Ajax's behaviour (758–77).

757 For this day only It is a convention in Greek tragedy that the action takes place over a single day (see 802). In Euripides' *Medea*, attention is drawn to this when Medea vows to kill three of her enemies in 'this one day'.

● What is the emotional effect on the audience of knowing that Athena's anger will last only one day?

758–61 Those fools Calchas's insight is similar to Athena's verdict in 127–33.

J.K. Stephen as Ajax in the 1882 Cambridge production.

CHORUS He is not in. He has just left,   735
    With fresh purpose, and in a new frame of mind.

MESSENGER *Iou iou!*
    Then I was sent on this errand too late,
    Or else it is I who have been too slow.

CHORUS What have we missed that is so vital?   740

MESSENGER Teucer ordered that he be kept indoors
    And not allowed out until he gets here himself.

CHORUS He is gone, and his mind is set on better things:
    To end his anger and appease the gods.

MESSENGER These words of yours are full of folly,   745
    If Calchas is a reliable prophet.

CHORUS Why? What do you know about this?

MESSENGER I know because I happened to be there.
    Calchas moved from the main circle of leaders
    And stood some way off from the sons of Atreus.   750
    He placed his hand on Teucer's in a friendly manner
    And warned him that he should keep Ajax
    Inside his tent by any means required
    For the present day, and not to let him
    Outside if he wished to see him alive again.   .755
    Divine Athena's anger would pursue him
    For this day only; that is what he said.
    'Those fools who are too great for their own good
    Are brought down by the gods with crushing blows –
    Anyone who, despite his mortal nature, fails   760
    To think like a man.' So the prophet spoke.

764–5 seek to win... with the help of heaven In the *Iliad*, victories won with divine help were regarded as more and not less glorious.

The arrogance (*hubris*) of Ajax

Earlier, Athena expressed the inescapable principle, underlying most of tragedy, that the arrogant or excessive must be brought down and made to suffer (the god Dionysus and the goddess Aphrodite say the same in the prologues of Euripides' *Bacchae* and *Hippolytus* respectively). Here, Calchas repeats the principle (758–61) and, at a moment when the audience must be wondering what Ajax is doing, we are given two examples of his past *hubris* (762–9 and 770–5).

Calchas' evidence of Ajax's past *hubris* suggests that it is an inherent character trait. His crime may therefore be seen as a symptom of his character.

The fact that Calchas could not possibly have witnessed a conversation between Ajax and his father in Salamis does not affect the validity of what he says. Greek tragedy places less importance on realism than much modern literature or theatre.

- Compare Ajax's treatment of Athena in Calchas' reported account (771–5) with his behaviour towards her in the prologue (91–117).
- What is the effect of Calchas' final remark in 778–9?

784–5 Poor Tecmessa, born to misery, come / And hear Tecmessa has not heard the messenger's speech. This suggests that she left the stage at 692 and re-enters now.

'But, as soon as he left home, Ajax proved
Himself a fool, despite his father's sound advice.
His father said to him: "Son, seek to win,
But always with the help of heaven."   765
And he replied, with arrogance and folly,
"Father, with the gods' help, a worthless man
Could gain a victory. I think I could win
The same success for myself without them."
Such was his boast. And then a second time,   770
When divine Athena was urging him
To turn his deadly hands against the enemy,
He made a terrible and blasphemous reply:
"Mistress, go and stand beside the other Greeks.
The line will never break where I am fighting."   775
By words like these he earned her ruthless fury,
With thoughts beyond the bounds of mortal man.
But if he should survive this day, then, god willing,
We may yet be the men who save him.'
Such were the prophet's words, and straight away   780
Teucer rose from his seat and sent me off
To give you this message. If we are foiled,
Then our man is no more, or Calchas is no prophet.
CHORUS Poor Tecmessa, born to misery, come
And hear what news this man has brought.   785
This matter touches us too close for comfort.
TECMESSA Why must you disturb me when I have just
Found peace from these unending troubles!

802 This very day means life or death for him See note on 757.

807 He has deceived me; I can see that now Whether or not Ajax was lying in his speech (see lines 652–9, 690–2), Tecmessa now believes that he wilfully deceived her.

Scene change
After 814 we have what effectively amounts to a brief interval. From here on, the action takes place elsewhere: in a remote place which, though still near the shore, is some distance away from the Greek camp (see 654–9).

The action of Greek tragedy usually takes place in a single fixed location. Changes of scene are very rare. Events which take place elsewhere are usually presented indirectly by means of messenger speeches (see note on Messenger speeches on page 52). The only other known example of a scene change is in Aeschylus' *Eumenides*, where less than a quarter of the way through the play the action moves from Delphi to Athens.

The Chorus and Tecmessa presumably rush off at 814, either together or, more likely, in different directions. The *orchēstra* and stage are left empty. This does not seem to occur anywhere else in known tragedy. In the ancient theatre, the total vacating of the stage may itself have been enough to indicate a change of scene, but the scenery may also have been changed.

The search for Ajax
Whenever Ajax is not on stage he is either being talked about or is the focus of a search. The situation here perhaps recalls Odysseus' search for Ajax in the prologue, but there are more differences than similarities. The present search takes place offstage and is concurrent with the scene which follows. In the prologue the primary focus was on the searcher; here it is on the man who is the object of the search.

o Explore ways of staging the following scene so that it is clear that Ajax makes his climactic monologue while the sailors are searching for him.

CHORUS Listen to this man. He is here
 With distressing news about Ajax.
TECMESSA *Oi moi!* What are you saying? Are we ruined?
MESSENGER Your fate I do not know, but as for Ajax,
 If he is not here, I do not hold out much hope.
TECMESSA He has gone out. Your words fill me with fear.
MESSENGER Teucer commands that he be kept   795
 Inside his tent and not let out alone.
TECMESSA Where is Teucer? Why is he saying this?
MESSENGER He has only just arrived, and he fears
 That if Ajax is gone it may prove fatal.
TECMESSA *Oi moi!* From whom did he hear this?   800
MESSENGER From Thestor's son, the prophet Calchas.
 This very day means life or death for him.
TECMESSA Save me, my friends, from the clutches of fate!
 Some of you, hurry, bring Teucer here quickly!
 Others go down to the bays, east and west,   805
 And follow Ajax's ill-omened trail.
 He has deceived me; I can see that now.
 I have lost the favour he used to show me.
 What shall I do, child? We must not sit idle.
 I will go as well, as far as I can. Come on!   810
 Hurry! There is no time to rest
 If we are to save a man who is set on death.
CHORUS We are ready, and will prove it
 Not just with words, but prompt action.

FOURTH EPISODE (815–65)

Ajax's final speech

Ajax enters. His sword is already fixed in the ground. In all other extant Greek tragedies, the only time characters may be alone on stage (without the Chorus) is during the prologue. This scene, in which Ajax delivers what is effectively a soliloquy in the middle of the play, is unique.

- What is the dramatic impact of Sophocles' break with dramatic convention here? (See notes on Scene change, page 58, and Staging Ajax's death, page 62, for other unconventional aspects of this play.)

817 The gift of Hector We now see the sinister irony of Ajax's earlier declaration (657–8) that he would bury Hector's sword; he is, in fact, going to bury it in his own body (see also note on lines 662–5).

The importance of burial

Ajax shows concern about the fate of his body (829–30). The ancient Greeks believed that without burial the soul could not rest in peace. This is why the unresolved fate of a dead hero's body is frequently a source of tension in epic and tragedy. In the *Iliad*, the Greeks fight zealously to rescue the body of Achilles' dearest friend Patroclus, and Priam risks death at the hands of Achilles to recover his son Hector's body. The plot of Sophocles' *Antigone* also hinges on Antigone's determination to bury her brother against the orders of King Creon.

Ajax's prayers

Ajax calls upon several gods in his final speech. First he asks his ancestor Zeus to ensure that he is found and buried (823–30). Next he calls on Hermes (832), one of whose roles in Greek religion was to lead the dead to the Underworld, to grant him a quick, painless death. After this he turns his thoughts to avenging his enemies. The Furies (837) were three immortal sisters – Alecto, Tisiphone and Megaera (commonly called the Eumenides, or 'The Kindly Ones', out of fear) – who avenged all human injustice. Finally, he asks Helios (846), the divine personification of the sun, to tell his parents of his misfortune. The reason for asking Helios is presumably that the sun travelled across the world in its daily course.

AJAX The executioner is set where it can cut
      Most cleanly, if there is time for such thoughts.
      The gift of Hector, whom I loathed so much,
      Whose sight I hated most of all my enemies,
      Is planted in this hostile Trojan soil,
      The blade just sharpened on a grinding stone.   820
      I have embedded it with care so that it may
      Oblige me kindly with an instant death.
      Everything is set. After this, O Zeus,
      Be first to help me, as is only right.
      It is a modest favour that I ask of you: 825
      To send a bearer of my grievous news to Teucer,
      That he may be the first to lift me up
      From where I fall on this freshly stained sword,
      So that I am not found first by some enemy
      And thrown as carrion to the dogs and birds.   830
      This, Zeus, is all I ask of you. I also call on
      Hermes, who guides the dead, to put me gently
      To rest, without a struggle, in one swift leap,
      Once I puncture my ribcage with this sword.
      And I ask the help of the ever-living maidens   835
      Who look for ever on all human suffering,
      The stern, far-ranging Furies. Let them mark
      How I am ruined by the sons of Atreus.
      Strike that evil pair with harshest evils!
      Obliterate them! And as they see me fallen   840
      From a self-inflicted blow, so let them perish
      At the hands of their own beloved children.
      Come, you Furies, swift avengers! Glut your rage!
      Do not spare a soul in the army! And you
      Who steer your chariot along high heaven,   845
      Helios, when you spy my native land,
      Check your reins, all laden with gold,
      And tell my aged father and poor mother
      Who raised me of my disastrous downfall.

852 But all such wailing is useless Ajax is hard-hearted to the end. After dwelling poignantly but briefly on his parents' grief, he reaffirms his resolute frame of mind.

854–8 Death, Death… never again! These lines are thought to be interpolated.

- Do Ajax's change of mind in 855 and the repetition of an invocation to Helios (846) suggest that the lines are inferior to the rest of the speech?

861 And glorious Athens, kindred race to mine Even at this climactic point in the play Sophocles reminds us of the close ties between Athens and Salamis (see note on Salamis, page 44).

Ajax's final farewell

Ajax thinks briefly of his parents before his final farewell to the world. Significantly, in his last lines he makes no mention of Tecmessa and Eurysaces, but focuses on the elements and the natural world.

- What qualities – positive or negative – does Ajax show in his final speech?
- What impression of Ajax are we left with?

Staging Ajax's death

After his speech Ajax falls on his sword. As a rule, deaths, and violence in general, took place offstage in tragedy (see note on Violence, page 26). But images of Ajax falling on his sword are common enough to suggest that this scene may, exceptionally, have been enacted on stage.

In Sophocles' day the number of actors with speaking parts was probably limited to three. The actor playing Ajax would therefore have to take another part after this scene. This means that Ajax's speech was almost certainly made on the *ekkyklēma*, but there is no sure way of knowing whether he was wheeled off before or after killing himself (see note on The discovery of Ajax, page 64).

FIFTH EPISODE (866–1184)

The Chorus re-enter at 866 in two groups, searching for Ajax. The section 866–78, during which both groups advance to the *orchēstra* at the front of the stage, is called the *epiparodos*. The section 878–973 is a passage of lament (*commus*). Lines 879–914 form a *strophē* to which 925–60 is the corresponding *antistrophē*.

Unhappy woman, when she hears the news
She will send a great cry throughout the city.
But all such wailing is useless. And now
The deed must be done and done quickly!
Death, Death, come gaze upon me now –
Wait, I will speak to you later below. 855
But you, light of this radiant day,
And Helios, in your chariot, I salute you
One last time and never again!
O light, O sacred soil of my birthplace,
Salamis, bedrock of my native hearth, 860
And glorious Athens, kindred race to mine,
You springs and rivers, and you plains of Troy,
You who have nursed me, I bid you farewell!
These are the last words Ajax has to say.
The rest I'll tell in Hades to the dead. 865

CHORUS (A) Toil brings only toil and more toil.
Where, where,
Where have I not tried?
Still no place reveals its secret.
Look, look! 870
Now I hear a noise!
CHORUS (B) It is us, your crewmen.
CHORUS (A) Any news?
CHORUS (B) We have looked everywhere west of the ships.
CHORUS (A) Did you find anything? 875
CHORUS (B) For all our efforts, not a thing.
CHORUS (A) Well, there is certainly no sign of him
Along the eastern side.

881–2 Or one of the nymphs / From Olympus There was a second
mountain called Olympus in Mysia. It seems likely that this is the
place the Chorus have in mind, as the gods' Olympus is in mainland
Greece, hundreds of miles from Troy.

The discovery of Ajax
The Chorus do not see Tecmessa until 894. She is presumably meant
to be concealed from them (and possibly the audience) by stage props.
Even when they spot her, the Chorus do not seem to see Ajax's body.
If the actor playing Ajax had to leave the stage at 866 (see note on
Staging Ajax's death, page 62), a dummy was presumably used to
represent Ajax's corpse in this scene. We may suppose that Tecmessa
appears on the *ekkyklēma* standing or kneeling over the dummy of
Ajax. There may have been foliage concealing the body at first, or
Tecmessa may have shielded it. In a contemporary production,
because there are no limitations on the number of actors, the scene
presents fewer problems.
○ Consider the most effective way of staging the play from 784 to 924.
○ What are the advantages of the corpse remaining in full view of the
audience for the rest of the play?

899 buried deep This eerily echoes the remark by Ajax in 658 about
burying his sword deep in the earth.

The Chorus' reaction to Ajax's death
The Chorus' first reaction is to think of the impact of Ajax's death on
themselves (900). Though fellow warriors, they are effectively
bystanders. They do, of course, express sorrow, but as Tecmessa later
says (942), their grief is not comparable to hers. In retrospect, they
comment that Ajax's death was inevitable (925–36).
● How consistent do you find the response of the Chorus from their
entry at 134 to this point of the play?

904 There is presumably a pause during which Tecmnessa composes
herself before saying 'What is done is done.'

CHORUS	If only some hard-working fisherman,
	Out on his sleepless quest,
	Or one of the nymphs
	From Olympus, or the flowing
	Streams of the Bosporus
	Could spy our harsh-tempered man,
	Wherever he is roaming,	885
	And call out to us.
	It is hard to have wandered
	So far, with all this effort,
	And met with no success. And still
	We cannot see where the ill-fated man is!	890

TECMESSA   *Io moi moi!*

CHORUS   Whose was that cry? It came from the grove nearby?

TECMESSA   *Io!* How terrible!

CHORUS   Look! I see Tecmessa, his poor
            Captive bride, deep in sorrow.   895

TECMESSA I'm crushed, ruined, destroyed, my friends.

CHORUS   Why? What is it?

TECMESSA Here lies Ajax, freshly killed, wrapped around
            A sword buried deep in his body.

CHORUS   *Oi moi!* So much for getting home!   900
            You have killed me too, my lord,
            Your fellow shipmate!
            Wretched man! Unhappy woman!

TECMESSA What is done is done. We can only weep.

CHORUS   With whose help did the poor man do this?   905

TECMESSA He clearly did it by himself. The sword
            He fell on is fixed in the ground; that proves it.

913–15 It is not clear when the Chorus see the body (see note on 1003).

914 with the ill-starred name See note on line 430.

920 What friend can carry you? By not removing the body to safety, the Chorus conform to the general rule, observed more strictly by Sophocles than Aeschylus or Euripides, that in tragedy the Chorus do not directly affect the action of the play.

Attic cup, showing Tecmessa covering Ajax's corpse (fifth century BC).

CHORUS   *Oi moi*, we are ruined!
You were bathed in blood,
Alone, unprotected by friends,
While we sensed nothing, and paid no attention,
Unaware of it all!
Where, where does Ajax lie,
The wilful man with the ill-starred name?

TECMESSA   None shall set eyes on him. No, I will wrap   915
Him in this robe and cover him completely.
No one who loves him could endure the sight.
Dark blood is gushing from the fatal cut,
And through his nose, from this self-inflicted wound.
What shall I do? What friend can carry you?   920
Where is Teucer? If only he were here,
Then he could tend his brother's body. Poor Ajax!
How mighty you were, how low you lie now!
A pitiful sight even to your enemies.

CHORUS   Poor hard-hearted man!   925
You were bound, bound,
In time, to meet an evil fate
Of untold suffering.
Such were the hateful words
You vented savagely,   930
All night and all day,
Against the sons of Atreus,
With deadly passion.
The day the contest was set up
For the arms of Achilles   935
Was the start of great misery.

4–5 *Io moi!*... in charge of us! Tecmessa's fear is one shared by many bereaved women in epic and tragedy, especially those plays or poems to do with Troy. Hector's wife Andromache in the *Iliad* shares Tecmessa's fear of an unkind Greek master (also see note on Homeric echoes, page 36).

Odysseus: the 'much-suffering hero'

Tecmessa sees Odysseus as Ajax's arch-enemy (953). The Chorus too, in 954–6, continue to regard him as the main instigator of ill-feeling towards Ajax (see 148–50, 187–9). They call him the **much-suffering hero** (955). This is one of the standard epithets for Odysseus in Homer's *Iliad* and *Odyssey*, but the phrase seems to be used ironically here: the Chorus imagine that the 'much-suffering' Odysseus cannot wait to tell Agamemnon and Menelaus and gloat over Ajax's ultimate suffering.

● Compare these perceptions of Odysseus with his actual behaviour in the play so far (see especially 121–6).

952 Zeus' daughter Pallas Pallas is another name for Athena.

957 *Pheu pheu!* This exclamation may express grief or anticipation.

Tecmessa's lament (961–73)

Tecmessa's lament is deeply moving. She shows a defiant spirit in her defence of Ajax. Her declaration that she feels more grief than his enemies do pleasure at Ajax's death underlines his greatness while belittling them.

● Is Tecmessa's speech in keeping with her character elsewhere?

TECMESSA	*Io moi moi!*
CHORUS	Noble grief pains the heart, I know.
TECMESSA	*Io moi moi!*
CHORUS	It is no surprise that you weep 940
	Twice over, robbed of one so dear.
TECMESSA	You can only imagine it. I feel it – all too keenly.
CHORUS	I understand.
TECMESSA	*Io moi*, my child, what harsh bondage we face!
	Such are the masters now in charge of us! 945
CHORUS	*Io moi*, it would be unspeakable
	If the two heartless sons of Atreus
	Were to do what you suggest
	In the midst of such distress. God forbid!

TECMESSA	Things would not be like this without the gods. 950
CHORUS	Then they have sent us pains too hard to bear.
TECMESSA	Such is the sorrow Zeus' daughter Pallas,
	That grim goddess, sows for Odysseus' sake.

CHORUS	I am sure in his black heart
	The 'much-suffering hero' gloats, 955
	Laughing out loud at our maddening grief.
	Pheu pheu! And that pair of kings,
	The sons of Atreus, will be
	Laughing with him, as soon as
	They hear what has happened. 960

TECMESSA	Well, let them laugh and rejoice at his suffering.
	They did not miss him when he was alive,
	But in the thick of battle they will rue his death.

974–6 *Io moi moi!* The entry of Teucer is heralded by his initial cry of distress (974) and by the Chorus' explicit mention of his arrival (975–6). The device of signalling characters' entries from the stage is partly to identify them and partly to allow them to cover the considerable distance from the side entrances (*parodoi*) in the ancient theatre, where they would first be visible, to the stage itself (see also 1042–6).

977 My dear beloved brother Ajax! Presumably Teucer sees the covered corpse at this point.

980 *Oi moi!* My fate is heavy indeed! Teucer's first thought, like the Chorus in 900, is of the effect of Ajax's death on himself.

981–3 Here Teucer and the Chorus speak in alternate half-lines.
- What is the effect of the half-lines here?

Evil-minded men do not know the good
That is in their grasp until it is lost.
His death is as bitter to me as it is sweet
To them, and a relief to him. What he desired
He made his own: the end he longed for.
Why, then, do they exult over this man?
He died at the hands of the gods, not theirs. 970
Well, let Odysseus have his hollow victory.
To them Ajax means nothing any more;
To me he is gone, leaving sorrow and tears.

TEUCER *(offstage) Io moi moi!*

CHORUS Quiet! I think I hear the voice of Teucer. 975
His cries appear to spring from this disaster.

TEUCER My dear beloved brother Ajax!
Have you fared as the rumour said?

CHORUS He is no more, Teucer, be sure of that.

TEUCER *Oi moi!* My fate is heavy indeed! 980

CHORUS So it would seem.

TEUCER   I'm ruined, ruined!

CHORUS We can but weep.

TEUCER   So rash an act!

CHORUS Too much so, Teucer!

TEUCER   But what of his son?
Where in Troy can I find him?

987 Like the cub of a lioness without a mate
● How appropriate is this simile?

988 Go! Hurry! Our manuscripts have no stage directions, but presumably Tecmessa leaves the stage at this point to find her son Eurysaces, since she reappears with him at 1168.

988–9 All men delight / In mocking a man who lies dead Ajax behaved in such a way towards the animals he believed were his enemies (302–4), and Athena invited an unwilling Odysseus to mock the possessed Ajax (79).

1003–4 This order is presumably addressed to the Chorus, who may now see the corpse for the first time.

1006 Where can I go now? To what people? It is usually female characters who express such fears when deprived of a husband or powerful male figure. Tecmessa does it earlier (see 510–19).
● What is the effect of Teucer behaving in a way which we might expect more from a female character?

Teucer and Telamon
Teucer's remarks about his father (1008–21) give us a fuller picture of Telamon than we have had so far. (See note on Telamon, page 32.)
● Compare what he says with Ajax's view of Telamon in 434–41.

1009–11 greet me kindly, with a cheerful look This is the first of several examples of Teucer's sense of irony.

CHORUS Alone by the tents.

TEUCER   Bring him here quickly,
In case one of our enemies snatches him up
Like the cub of a lioness without a mate.
Go! Hurry! Get to work! All men delight
In mocking a man who lies dead.

CHORUS Before he died Ajax asked that you   990
Protect his son, as you are doing now.

TEUCER Of all that my eyes have ever beheld
This to me is the sorriest of sights! The path
That pained my heart the most, of all the roads
That I have ever taken, is the one I followed   995
Now, dearest Ajax, when, tracking you down,
I came to learn the manner of your death.
A rumour so swift that it seemed from the gods
Reached all the Greeks, that you were dead and gone.
I heard it when I was some way off, and I groaned   1000
In pain. But now the sight of you destroys me!
Oi moi!
Come, unveil him and let me see the worst.
Face of grim courage, so hard to behold!
What sorrows you have sown for me by dying.   1005
Where can I go now? To what people?
I who did nothing to help in your hour of need?
I am sure that Telamon, your father and mine,
Will greet me kindly, with a cheerful look,
When I return without you. Of course he will,   1010
The man who never even smiles when fate is kind!

)13 the bastard sprung from his war prize Teucer refers to himself as an illegitimate child because his mother Hesione, like Tecmessa, was a Trojan captive given to his father as a prize. In speaking of himself in such disparaging terms, Teucer is imagining Telamon's viewpoint. The speech marks in lines 1014–16 indicate what Teucer anticipates Telamon saying to him.

1019–20 And in the end... instead of a free man Exile meant a total loss of social status and rights. To the Greeks, being a free citizen was an essential part of their existence. In Euripides' *Medea*, as a foreigner living in Corinth, one of Medea's main complaints is about being stateless. In Sophocles' *Philoctetes*, being stateless is a form of living death.

1028–39 The authenticity of these lines has been questioned.
● Explore possible reasons for doubting these lines.

1029 By the belt he was given See note on 662–5.

1040 Keep your words brief! The Chorus' words and tone suggest that Teucer commands less respect than Ajax. One imagines that the Chorus would never have urged Ajax to cut short a speech.

The arrival of Menelaus
1042–6 Menelaus' entry is signalled in much the same way, and for the same reason, as Teucer's at 974 (see note on 974–6).

What will he hold back? What taunt will he not use
Against the bastard sprung from his war prize?
'He betrayed you with spineless cowardice,
Dearest Ajax, or by deceit, hoping to take
Your place in the household once you were dead.'
Such will be his words, the ill-tempered man,
Stern in old age and quick to wrangle over nothing.
And in the end, I will be thrown out, driven from
The land, and dubbed a slave instead of a free man.
Such is my fate at home. While here at Troy
My enemies abound and help is scarce;
What I had has disappeared with your death.
Oi moi! What should I do? How can I draw you
From the cruel point of this gleaming sword,
The executioner to whom you breathed your last?
See how dead Hector was meant to kill you!
Look, in god's name, upon the fates of these
Two men! By the belt he was given by this man,
Hector was strapped to a chariot rail
And mangled until he gasped out his life.
And from Hector Ajax received this gift
And died upon it with a fatal fall.
Surely a Fury wrought this sword,
And Hell that war belt – a grim craftsman!
I would say that these things, like everything,
Are engineered for mortals by the gods.
Whoever disagrees with this idea,
May he cherish his view as I do mine.
CHORUS Keep your words brief! Decide how you will bury
The man, and what you will have to say then.
I see one of our enemies. Perhaps he comes
To mock our troubles, as evil men do.

1020

1025

1030

1035

1040

〕45 the man for whom we made this voyage Menelaus is so described because he is Helen's husband. The main purpose of the Greek expedition to Troy was to recover Helen.

1050 the commander of the army i.e. Agamemnon.

The first *agon* (1047–1162)

After Teucer's speech there is a marked change in atmosphere. The solemnity and sorrow in the wake of Ajax's death give way to pettiness and wrangling. The quarrel is over Ajax's body. Conflict over the burial of a hero is a recurring theme in Greek myth and literature (see note on The importance of burial, page 60).

A formal debate (*agon*) is a conventional feature of Greek tragedy. Athenians were extraordinarily fond of all forms of debate. It was a prevalent feature of fifth-century Athenian political and legal life. All citizens had a right to participate in the assembly and to serve as jurors. Some kind of *agon* occurs in most extant plays. It may consist of long speeches, quick-fire dialogue or, as here, a mixture of both. The *agon* is also a feature of Greek comedy.

Menelaus in Homer

In the *Iliad* Menelaus is portrayed as a brave and honourable warrior. In the *Odyssey* he is characterised similarly but is shown as genial and slightly blundering. Tragedians freely changed characters from how they appear in Homer (see note on The character of Odysseus, page 6). In most of his appearances in tragedy Menelaus is portrayed as an unpleasant, unscrupulous or, at best, ridiculous character (as in Euripides' *Andromache* and *Helen*).

● What initial impression do we get of Menelaus in this play?

1067–70 We could not control him... a word I said Menelaus' suggestion that Ajax does not listen to others is consistent with what Calchas was reported as having said earlier (see 762–75). There is no suggestion of unruliness on Ajax's part in the *Iliad*; it may therefore be a Sophoclean invention.

TEUCER And who is it, this warrior that you see?

CHORUS Menelaus, the man for whom we made this voyage.

TEUCER I see him. He's not hard to make out at this range.

MENELAUS You there! I warn you not to lift a finger
To move that body. Leave it where it is.

TEUCER Why waste your breath on such an order?

MENELAUS I will it; so does the commander of the army.   1050

TEUCER And can you tell me what your reasons are?

MENELAUS When we led him from home, we hoped that he
Would be a friend and ally to the Greeks. Instead
We have found him more hostile than the Trojans.
He intended to murder the whole army,   1055
Coming by at night to put us to the sword.
And if a god had not foiled his attempt
We would have met the fate that is now his –
Lying low in a miserable death –
While he survived. But as things are, a god   1060
Deflected his assault onto our sheep and cattle.
For this reason no man has power enough
To lay his body to rest in a grave. Instead,
He will be cast out on the yellow sand
To become food for the birds of the shore.   1065
Raise no angry threats in response to this.
We could not control him when he was alive,
But now he is dead we shall rule him with a firm hand,
Whether you like it or not. While he lived
He never listened to a word I said.   1070

71–2 Ajax is a **common man** only in the sense that he is not one of the two supreme commanders of the combined Greek army. The use of such a demeaning phrase for a hero who is the ruler of Salamis tells us more about Menelaus than Ajax.

Menelaus' speech

The political system, in Menelaus' view (1071–86), is indistinguishable from the military system: a chain of command with himself and Agamemnon at the head of it. Such a political system may well have seemed like tyranny to most of the fifth-century Athenians who made up Sophocles' original audience and were governed by a radical democracy. For them, democracy was a fundamental right.

The presentation of Menelaus may itself be politically motivated. Menelaus was king of Sparta. In the Spartan constitution, power lay in the hands of a small governing body headed by two soldier-kings. At the probable date of the play, Athens and Sparta were either at war or on the brink of war. The situation in Sparta was not all that dissimilar from that of the Greeks at Troy.

- What points does Menelaus make? What do his arguments and manner suggest about his character?
- What does the Chorus' response to Menelaus tell us about him?

1091–2 Menelaus, you have set out wise principles The Chorus, as is often the case in tragedy, adopt a mediating role in the *agon* (see also 1118–19).

Teucer's response

Teucer begins by questioning the link between high birth and personal virtue. He then attempts to answer Menelaus' points in the manner of a debate.

- Which points does he answer effectively and which does he overlook?
- What is Teucer's attitude and manner towards Menelaus?

It is a mark of evil when a common man
Will not heed those in charge of him.
The laws of state can never function freely,
Not unless fear is properly in place.
Nor can an army be sensibly led   107.
Without a curtain of fear and respect.
A man must realise, however strong he is,
That he may fall to the gentlest of blows.
If he maintains a sense of fear and shame,
Be sure that such a man will remain safe.   1080
But where insolence and licence are rife,
Such a state, though sailing smoothly at first,
Will one day plummet to the very depths.
So let me see fear in its rightful place,
And let us not hope to act as we please   1085
Without later paying the price in pain.
These things go by turns. In the past this man
Blazed with disrespect. Now it's is my turn to be proud.
Therefore I warn you, do not bury him, in case
By doing so you earn yourself a grave.   1090

CHORUS Menelaus, you have set out wise principles,
But do not yourself show disrespect to the dead.

TEUCER I'll never be surprised again if someone
Of no account does wrong, when those
Who seem to be of noble birth can go so far   1095
Astray in what they say. Come, tell me from
The start again. You say you brought
This man here as an ally of the Greeks?
Did he not sail here of his own accord?

11–14 He did not come here to fight on your wife's / Behalf
An oath was taken by all those who came to seek the hand of Helen that they would all support the successful suitor in recovering her if she were ever abducted.

1114 He did not care for nobodies There is irony here as the men he is referring to are in fact the joint commanders of the Greek army.

1115–16 Next time… bring more heralds / And the commander
Teucer's remark perhaps suggests that he wants to see more pomp and ceremony before he will listen to what is being said. It is also an insult to Menelaus, and one which anticipates the arrival of Agamemnon, the **commander**.

1118–19 Despite being fellow Salaminians, the Chorus are objective in accordance with their role as mediators (see note on 1091–2).

1120 It seems the bowman has no lack of pride Teucer was known as a bowman, considered inferior to those who carried a shield and fought with spear and sword (1122). In the *Iliad* he fights in tandem with Ajax, firing his arrows from behind Ajax's great shield.

1120–41 After the two main speeches of the *agon* there follows a section of *stichomythia* (see note on page 4).
● How is the device used to dramatic effect here?
● How does the atmosphere created by this sort of verbal sparring compare with the overall atmosphere of the first half of the play?

Attic vase painting showing Ajax carrying Achilles' body.

What right have you to command him? What right
Have you to lead the men he brought from home?
You came as Sparta's leader, not our master.
No law says that you have power over him
Any more than he has power over you.
You sailed here as leader of a detachment,   1105
Not commander-in-chief; you never led Ajax.
Rule your own people! Use your pompous words
To lecture them. But as for him, whatever you
Or that other general say, I will bury him
As is my right. Your words do not scare me.   1110
He did not come here to fight on your wife's
Behalf, like your overworked subjects.
No, he came because he was bound by oath,
Not for your sake – he did not care for nobodies.
Next time you come here bring more heralds –   1115
And the commander. I pay no attention
To your ranting, so long as you are what you are.
CHORUS I dislike such a tone in times of trouble:
No matter how fair, harsh words sting.
MENELAUS It seems the bowman has no lack of pride.   1120
TEUCER The art I practise is no mean one.
MENELAUS How proudly you'd boast if you owned a shield!
TEUCER Shield or not I could match you fully armed.
MENELAUS That tongue of yours nurses a fearsome heart!
TEUCER A man with justice on his side can afford to be proud.   1125

32 A public enemy; it would be wrong to bury him One definition of virtue among the Greeks, later famously expressed and challenged in Plato's *Republic*, is 'helping one's friends and harming one's enemies'. Despite the fact that respecting the rights of the dead is an extremely important aspect of Greek religion, Menelaus gives priority to the second half of this principle. Similarly, in Sophocles' *Antigone*, Creon refused burial to Antigone's brother Polyneices (his own nephew) because he was a traitor.

1135 You were caught stealing votes from him Teucer and Menelaus are referring to the voting for who should receive the arms of Achilles. Teucer accuses Menelaus of rigging votes.

● How convincing is Menelaus' denial?

The end of the first *agon*

Menelaus tries to end matters with a kind of parable, which he bluntly explains before delivering a parting insult. But Teucer responds with a mocking parable of his own. He refuses to let Menelaus have the last word and, ignoring his final threat, taunts him as he departs.

● How is Teucer's defiant spirit brought out in the debate so far?
● Whose arguments are the more persuasive?
● Who seems the more quick-witted of the two?

MENELAUS Is it right for my killer to be honoured?

TEUCER Killer? A miracle! He killed you, yet you live!

MENELAUS A god saved me. To Ajax I was dead.

TEUCER Then do not dishonour the gods, if they saved you.

MENELAUS What? How could I offend the laws of heaven? 1130

TEUCER By coming here to stop a dead man being buried.

MENELAUS A public enemy; it would be wrong to bury him.

TEUCER Did Ajax ever declare war on you?

MENELAUS We hated one another. You knew that.

TEUCER You were caught stealing votes from him. 1135

MENELAUS He was tricked by the judges, not by me.

TEUCER You'd shroud any number of crimes in secrecy.

MENELAUS Someone will suffer for those words.

TEUCER No more, I think, than the pain I will inflict.

MENELAUS I will say one thing: he must not be buried. 1140

TEUCER And I say this: he shall be buried!

MENELAUS I once saw a man with a ready tongue
Urging some seamen to sail in a storm.
But in the thick of it, you could not hear
A sound from him, as he hid underneath 1145
His cloak, letting the crew walk over him at will.
So too with your loud mouth: a mighty storm
Blowing up from some tiny cloud
Will quickly put an end to all your shouting.

163 a mighty contest is under way The Chorus comment upon the action. The Greek word for 'contest' is *agon*, which also means 'debate' (see note on The first *agon*, page 76). The term 'contest' may be describing both the action within the play and the first *agon* itself as a formal dramatic feature. If so, this implies a kind of awareness, on the part of the Chorus, of the fact that they are in a play. Moments of self-reference are rare in tragedy, though very frequent in comedy. The remark also suggests that the quarrel is not yet over, and that we may expect another confrontation (see also 1115–16).

Staging the *agon*

In Sophocles' day, there was a close link between the military and political worlds: often, politicians were also generals. Sophocles himself held high office.

In one professional production in London the characters in the *agon* were all played as French politicians. In another professional production in New York, all the male characters were played as modern US soldiers.

● How appropriate or effective might such approaches be?
○ Explore ways of staging the quarrel to bring out the differences in character of the combatants and to heighten dramatic tension.

Arrival of Tecmessa and Eurysaces

Menelaus departs at 1160. Tecmessa and Eurysaces come on stage at 1168. They do not speak (see note on Staging Ajax's death, page 62) but participate in certain funeral rites (1169–70). The temporary air of solemnity contrasts sharply with the noise and rancour of the preceding scene and the scene to come.

Funeral rites

The ancient Greeks practised burial and cremation. Heroes in the *Iliad* were usually cremated and their ashes buried in a grave or tomb. The first stage of the funerary rites consisted of laying out the body, anointing it and dressing it with flowers. In their current predicament, Tecmessa and Eurysaces can do little more than remain beside the body in supplication (1170–2), in case their enemies should try to remove it. Teucer must go alone to prepare a resting place (1183–4). All three offer locks of hair as a token of supplication (1173–5). Suppliants were under the protection of Zeus, and violation of this protection was seen as the utmost sacrilege.

TEUCER Well, I once saw a man full of folly
    Who gloated over others in distress.
    Then somebody like me saw him
    And said something like this:
    'Do not commit evil against the dead,
    For if you do, be sure you will regret it.'   1155
    This was how he warned the misguided man.
    But wait, I see him, and he is, I think,
    None other than you! Do I speak in riddles?
MENELAUS I'll go. I'd feel ashamed if someone heard
    That I sparred with words when I could use force.   1160
TEUCER Be off! It is far more shameful for me
    To listen to a foolish man's abuse.
CHORUS A mighty contest is under way.
    Quick as you can, Teucer,
    Hurry and seek a hollow grave   1165
    For Ajax, where he can rest
    In a dank tomb, remembered for ever!
TEUCER And look, his wife and child are here
    In time to prepare his poor corpse
    For burial. Come here, my child, and stand   1170
    Beside him, touch the father who begot you,
    As a suppliant. And now turn yourself
    Towards him and kneel, with these locks of hair
    In your hands: mine, hers and your own –
    The suppliant's offering. And if a warrior   1175
    Should try to tear you by force from this corpse
    May his evil bring him to an evil end – cast
    From the earth unburied, his whole lineage severed
    At the root, as I cut off this lock of hair.

82 And you, don't stand around like women! The Chorus has in
fact shown its concern and support in 118–19 and 1164–7.

● What does Teucer's reprimand tell us about his state of mind?

THIRD CHORAL ODE (3RD *STASIMON*) (1185–1222)

The final choral ode comprises two pairs of corresponding stanzas.
After despairing at the length of the Trojan expedition (1185–91), the
Chorus deliver a categorical condemnation of war as a whole
(1192–8). Such an anti-war stance is not uncommon in tragic choral
odes, especially in plays connected with the Trojan story (for example,
Aeschylus' *Agamemnon* and Euripides' *Trojan Women*).

In the first of the second pair of stanzas (1199–1210), the Chorus
list the hardships of war and, for the first time, the joys of peace.

● What is the effect of mentioning peacetime joys here?

1191 To the sorrow and shame of Greece The Chorus imply that the
very idea of coming to retrieve Helen is shameful.

1192 If only the man This sort of wishful thinking is not uncommon
in Greek tragedy. Euripides' *Medea* famously opens with the line, 'If
only the *Argo* had never winged its way'.

Courtesy, Museum of Fine Arts, Boston. Reproduced with permission.
© 2000 Museum of Fine Arts, Boston. All rights reserved.

Greek vase from the sixth century BC depicting Ajax's suicide.

Hold him, my boy, and guard him; let no one
Move you. Kneel beside him and cling to him.
And you, don't stand around like women!
At least protect him until I return from
Making a grave, though all the world forbid me.

CHORUS   What will be the last,   1185
                    When will the tally of restless
                        Years cease; years which
                    Always bring me the unending
                    Sufferings of war throughout
                        The wide plain of Troy,   1190
                    To the sorrow and shame of Greece?

                    If only the man who first taught
                        The Greeks allied warfare,
                        With its hateful weapons,
                    Had vanished into the wide sky   1195
                        Or all-receiving Hades.
                    O sorrow, bringer of sorrows!
                    He was the wrecker of mankind!

                    It was he who denied me
                        The pleasure of garlands   1200
                    And deep-filled cups of wine,
                        The sweet sound of flutes,
                    And the delight of sleep at night,
                        Much to my sorrow.
                    And love! He has kept me   1205
                    From love! I lie here like this,
                        Cared for by no one,
                    My hair always matted
                        With heavy dew,
                    A reminder of cheerless Troy.   1210

211–22 In the final stanza the Chorus imagine being transported far from Troy back to Greece, close to their native Salamis. Such escapism features in other choral odes (the Chorus in Euripides' *Bacchae*, for example, at one point express a desire to be transported away from Thebes to Cyprus). Choral odes often shift in this way from the real to the imaginary or from the particular to the general.

1211–12 Before, brave Ajax / Was always my defence
- Where else has the Chorus' dependence on Ajax been expressed?

1217–18 O to be beneath / The cliff tops of Sunium Sunium is a promontory on the southern tip of Attica, the district around Athens. A famous temple of Poseidon is situated there (see map on page vii).

EXODOS (1223–1418)
This was the name given to the final section of the play.

The second *agon* (1226–1315)
After the choral ode Agamemnon arrives, without Menelaus, to confront Teucer. There is an awkward entry at 1223, as Teucer seems to rush on stage ahead of Agamemnon. Teucer's comment in 1225, whether or not it is heard by Agamemnon, reaffirms his spirit of defiance.

Agamemnon in Homer
In the *Iliad*, Agamemnon is portrayed as a brave warrior, but an aggressive, quarrelsome leader. Most of the action in the *Iliad* is the consequence of a quarrel between Agamemnon and Achilles.
- What impression do we gain of Agamemnon from the style and language of his first remarks, and what is his attitude to Teucer?

1228 slave woman's son Teucer's parents were, in fact, both of the highest birth (see note on Telamon, page 32, and lines 1299–1303).

1234 You say Ajax sailed here Agamemnon must have been informed of what Teucer said to Menelaus earlier (1099).

Before, brave Ajax
Was always my defence
Against nightly fears
And the enemy's arrows.
Now he is lost to an evil fate.   1215
What joy, what joy remains
For me? O to be beneath
The cliff tops of Sunium,
Where the wooded cape juts out
To sea, pounded by the waves,   1220
From where we could
Salute sacred Athens.

TEUCER I rushed back because I saw the commander
  Agamemnon heading this way towards us.
  I'm sure he will give his foul mouth full rein.   1225
AGAMEMNON It is you, they say, that have dared to spout
  Dangerous words against us with impunity!
  I am talking to you, slave woman's son!
  If you were the child of a well-born mother,
  No doubt you'd use fine words and strut on high,   1230
  Since as one nobody you stand up for another,
  Swearing solemnly that we are not leaders
  Of the Greek army or the fleet.
  You say Ajax sailed here as his own man.
  Is it not a scandal to hear such talk from slaves?   1235
  What was this man you boast of with such pride?
  Where did he go or take his stand that I did not?
  Are there no other men among the Greeks but him?

250–4 **It is not the thick-set, / Broad-shouldered men** Though he does not say so explicitly, Agamemnon seems to be contrasting Ajax with the likes of Odysseus here.

● What might Agamemnon's preference for **men of good sense** over **thick-set, broad-shouldered men** and the image in 1253–4 tell us about him as a leader?

1262–3 **When you speak… barbarian tongue** Agamemnon tops his previous insult with an even more outrageous jibe. He suggests that Teucer's speech is incomprehensible on account of his Trojan mother. Teucer is a Greek speaker and, in any case, the Trojans and Greeks share the same language and gods in tragedy, just as they do in Homeric epic.

Agamemnon's speech

Agamemnon re-emphasises the points made by Menelaus (compare 1246–9 with 1073–6), taking every opportunity to insult Teucer in the process. He makes abusive remarks about Teucer's parentage (1228–31, 1235, 1259–60) and belittles Ajax's military achievements (1237–8).

● Compare Agamemnon and Menelaus in terms of the views they express and their tone.

● What new points does Agamemnon make?

Teucer's reply to Agamemnon

Teucer begins his reply to Agamemnon with an address to the dead Ajax in which he wistfully laments Agamemnon's ingratitude towards him.

It seems that we shall rue the day we called
The Greeks to contest the arms of Achilles
If we are denounced by Teucer at every turn,
And if you are still not prepared, though beaten,
To bow to the decision of the judges,
But must keep on hurling abuse and stabbing
Us in the back – those of you that are left.   1245
Where such behaviour is allowed,
No law can be established properly;
Not if we thrust aside those who win fairly
And bring to the fore those who come behind.
Such things must be stopped! It is not the thick-set,   1250
Broad-shouldered men that can be counted on;
It is men of good sense who flourish everywhere.
An ox with a large frame can still
Be kept in line by a small whip.
I see such medicine in store for you   1255
Unless you acquire some wisdom. You boldly
Insult us with a ready tongue, even though
This man is no more, but already a ghost.
Have you no sense? Remember who you are!
Bring somebody else here – a freeborn man –   1260
And let him speak to us on your behalf.
When you speak, I can't understand:
I cannot interpret your barbarian tongue.
CHORUS May you both have the sense to show restraint.
I have no more advice for you than this.   1265
TEUCER Ah, Ajax, how quickly men's gratitude
To the dead slips away and is found treacherous,
If this man no longer remembers you,
Not even a little; the man for whom
You often toiled so hard, risking your life.   1270
But all that is forgotten, cast aside!

.273–82 Teucer recalls the episode in *Iliad xii* in which Hector drove the Greeks back to their own ships. Ajax led the counter-attack which saved the Greeks.

1283 when he met Hector face to face This took place in *Iliad vii*. See note on lines 662–5.

1285–7 It was no coward's token… the crested helmet When lots were drawn, participants would put a distinctively shaped piece of earth into a helmet and, when it was shaken, the first to fly out was the winner. Those not keen to fight might put in a damp clod that was unlikely to emerge, but not Ajax.

The house of Atreus

The royal house of Atreus was founded by Pelops (see line 1292). His son Atreus, father of Agamemnon and Menelaus, ruled a greater area than Telamon and Peleus, who both belonged to the house of Aeacus.

The family history of the house of Atreus was particularly gruesome. Pelops' father Tantalus killed him and fed him to the gods – he was subsequently restored to life. Atreus murdered his brother Thyestes' sons, and served them up to Thyestes in a feast (see lines 1293–4). A later son of Thyestes, Aegisthus, was the lover of Clytemnestra, Agamemnon's wife. Aegisthus avenged his father when he and Clytemnestra murdered Agamemnon upon his return from Troy (see Aeschylus' *Agamemnon*). Agamemnon's mother, Aerope, was Cretan (see line 1295). Her story also involved sexual misdemeanour and murder.

1302 Laomedon The former king of Troy (see note on Telamon, page 32, and Background to the story, pages v–vi).

Do you, who have just now spoken all those
Foolish words, have no memory of the time
When you were shut up within your defences,
Reduced to nothing as the battle turned?   127.
He came alone and rescued you when flames
Were roaring round the stern decks of the ships,
And all the while Hector was leaping high
Over the ditches and onto the hulls.
Who averted that? Was that not his doing –   1280
The man who, you claim, never stood where you
Did not? Would you admit he did his duty there?
Again, when he met Hector face to face,
Chosen by lot, not at any man's request,
It was no coward's token he threw in, no damp   1285
Clod of earth, but the sort that would be first
To leap lightly out of the crested helmet.
These were his deeds and I was there with him –
The slave, the son of a barbarian mother.
You fool! Are you blind when you say such things?   1290
Do you not know that the father of your father,
Old Pelops, was a barbarian – a Phrygian?
And Atreus, your father, gave his brother
A most unholy feast: the flesh of his own children!
You yourself were born of a Cretan mother,   1295
Whose father, when he caught her with a lover,
Sentenced her to be thrown as prey to silent fish.
Can such a man as you insult a pedigree
Like mine? The father I spring from is Telamon,
Who, as the army's highest prize for valour, won   1300
My mother as his bedfellow, and she was born
A princess, daughter of Laomedon.
Heracles gave her to him as a special gift.

Teucer's defence of Ajax

Teucer goes systematically through Agamemnon's charges and implied criticisms, as he did with Menelaus.

- What are the main points Teucer makes, and how thoroughly and successfully does he refute Agamemnon's accusations and insults?
- In the end, how convincing is Teucer's overall defence of Ajax?
- What positive characteristics does Teucer display in the course of his defence of Ajax?

1310–12 I would willingly die… for him rather than / Your wife – I mean your brother's wife This deliberate slip is an example of Teucer's ready wit. He may be implying that he does not care which of the sons of Atreus is married to Helen, or that Agamemnon champions Helen's cause so keenly as to make one forget that Menelaus is her husband, not him.

- What other signs are there of ready wit in this or the first *agon*?

The arrival of Odysseus

The second *agon* ends at 1315, after Teucer's speech, with the sudden arrival of Odysseus (1316). The *agon* is again inconclusive. We are left wondering what might have happened if Odysseus had not intervened.

- Is the quarrel fundamentally about Ajax's character or his crime?
- Is Teucer's position weakened by his conspicuous silence, in both confrontations, about Ajax's attempt to murder the Greek leaders?
- How much closer are Menelaus, Agamemnon and Teucer to resolving the issue of what is to happen to Ajax's body?

1316 … just in time The Chorus hope that Odysseus has come to make peace; a surprising reaction in view of their earlier criticisms of him (see 148–50, 187–9, 954–60). But in the *Iliad*, Odysseus was known as a shrewd mediator.

1330–1 I count / You as my greatest friend among the Greeks In the *Iliad,* Odysseus acts as a loyal friend to Agamemnon throughout his conflict with Achilles (see note on 1250–4).

As a noble son born of noble parents,
Would I disgrace my kinsman – a man whom you
Would cast out unburied – now that he lies
Low in misfortune, and not blush to say so?
Well, be sure of this: if you throw him out,
You will be throwing out our three corpses to lie
With him. I would willingly die in front of   1310
Everyone, fighting for him rather than
Your wife – I mean your brother's wife.
So think not just of me but of yourself.
If you harm me at all, you'll soon wish you
Had been a coward rather than a bully.   1315

CHORUS Lord Odysseus, you have come just in time,
    If you are here to help, not to make matters worse.

ODYSSEUS What is it? From far off I heard the sons of Atreus
    Shouting over this brave man's corpse.

AGAMEMNON I have had to listen to the most shameful words   1320
    Just now, lord Odysseus, from this man here.

ODYSSEUS What words? I can forgive a man
    Who trades insults when he suffers abuse.

AGAMEMNON He deserved it. His conduct towards me was shameful.

ODYSSEUS What has he done to cause you such offence?   1325

AGAMEMNON He says that he will not leave this man's corpse
    Unburied, but will honour it against my will.

ODYSSEUS Is it possible for a friend to speak the truth
    And still remain on good terms as before?

AGAMEMNON Speak, or else I would be a fool; I count   1330
    You as my greatest friend among the Greeks.

342–3 You cannot dishonour him justly Odysseus stresses the fact that to deny Ajax a burial would be simultaneously unjust and offensive to the gods.
- How surprising is Odysseus' response?

1348 So why not stamp all over him now that he's dead? This resembles Athena's suggestion to Odysseus at the beginning of the play (79). Of all the characters in the play, Odysseus alone expresses tolerance and pity towards fallen enemies.

1350 It isn't easy for a ruler to show reverence Agamemnon makes no secret of his urge to flout piety because of his position.

1358 Such is the way with fickle men!
- Does this expose Odysseus' fickleness or Agamemnon's narrow-mindedness?

Treatment of enemies
After gaining Agamemnon's consent to speak freely, Odysseus advocates tolerance and respect for the dead. He says that by not gloating over the dead, Agamemnon will be showing nobility.

The conflict between Agamemnon's and Odysseus' respective outlooks reflects contemporary philosophical debate about the nature of justice. Agamemnon believes we should be clear about who our friends and enemies are, and help our friends and harm our enemies. Odysseus says that we should act justly in all situations because friends and enemies may change (1359) – a sentiment expressed by Ajax, whether heartfelt or otherwise, in his penultimate speech (679–80). Ajax, he argues, had nobility; he was a friend before becoming an enemy, and now that he is dead he should be treated with due respect.
- Is this position consistent with Odysseus' outlook in the prologue (see especially lines 121–2)?

1359 Many who are enemies now Two major themes of the play are the transformative power of time and man's inability to foresee the future. (See also 131–2, 646–9, 1416–18.) Odysseus displays his intelligence and wisdom in this play through his understanding of this idea (see 1365).

ODYSSEUS Listen, then. In heaven's name, don't dare cast
This man out in cold blood without a burial!
You must not let violence make you hate
The man so much that you trample on justice.   133_
He was also my worst enemy in the army,
Ever since I won the arms of Achilles.
Be that as it may, I would not seek to
Dishonour Ajax by denying that
In him I saw the best of all the Greeks   1340
Who came to Troy, apart from Achilles.
You cannot dishonour him justly;
You would harm not him, but the laws of heaven.
Even if you hate him, it is not right
To harm a noble man once he is dead.   1345

AGAMEMNON Odysseus, are you taking his side against me?

ODYSSEUS I am. I hated him when it was right to hate.

AGAMEMNON So why not stamp all over him now that he's dead?

ODYSSEUS Son of Atreus, don't delight in unfair advantage.

AGAMEMNON It isn't easy for a ruler to show reverence.   1350

ODYSSEUS But he should value friends who offer sound advice.

AGAMEMNON A worthy man should obey those in charge.

ODYSSEUS Enough! You win by yielding to your friends.

AGAMEMNON Remember what sort of man you are supporting.

ODYSSEUS He was my enemy, but he was noble once.   1355

AGAMEMNON What would you do? Honour an enemy's corpse?

ODYSSEUS To me his virtue far outweighs our hatred.

AGAMEMNON Such is the way with fickle men!

ODYSSEUS Many who are enemies now are later friends.

Odysseus' mediation

Before proposing any solution to the crisis, Odysseus begins by asking Agamemnon a series of questions to establish exactly what the quarrel is about (1318–29). He also showed this tendency to suspend judgement until he has examined evidence in the prologue (see 21–3).

- How does Odysseus exploit his good relations with Agamemnon to get across his point of view?

Despite looking set to concede by line 1360, Agamemnon cannot help continuing to criticise Odysseus, before finally giving in.

- Examine the dialogue in lines 1346–69. How does the use of *stichomythia* highlight the contrast in character and style of the two speakers?
- What qualities does Odysseus show in dealing with Agamemnon? How does his manner and tone differ from that of Teucer, Menelaus and Agamemnon?

Odysseus finally persuades Agamemnon to relent by picking exactly the right moment to surprise him with bluntly presented hard moral facts rather than using his more customary tactful and diplomatic approach.

- How might a change in atmosphere from Odysseus' entry at 1318 be shown on stage?

1366–7 Every man for himself Odysseus' reason for pitying Ajax – that he will one day be in the same condition – is dismissed by Agamemnon as selfish. We may prefer to see it as enlightened self-interest, such as he shows in the prologue (see especially lines 121–6 and note on 1359).

1373 But do as you see fit! Agamemnon remains implacable towards Ajax, but says that he gives way out of regard for Odysseus.

- Is this the real reason, or is there another explanation for why Agamemnon is forced to concede to Odysseus?

1374–5 Odysseus alone, of the four men who speak in the quarrel, receives praise from the Chorus.

Teucer's reaction

Teucer thanks Odysseus for his successful mediation and goodwill towards Ajax, but reaffirms his hatred of Agamemnon and Menelaus (1389–92). This ill-will shows that he has not been converted to a more enlightened view, but maintains the same blunt creed as Agamemnon, Menelaus and Ajax, namely, that evil should be repaid with evil.

AGAMEMNON You recommend making friends of such men?

ODYSSEUS I do not recommend a stubborn spirit.

AGAMEMNON But you will make us seem cowards today.

ODYSSEUS All the Greeks will see you as fair.

AGAMEMNON So you are asking me to let this corpse be buried?

ODYSSEUS I am. One day I too will be in his position.   1365

AGAMEMNON Always the same! Every man for himself.

ODYSSEUS Who else should I think of, if not myself?

AGAMEMNON Then let this be called your doing, not mine.

ODYSSEUS However you arrange it, you will have done well.

AGAMEMNON You can be sure that I would grant you   1370
An even greater favour than this. As for him,
Whether here or below the ground, I shall
Always hate him. But do as you see fit!

CHORUS Odysseus, if any man says that you,
With your qualities, lack wisdom, he is a fool.   1375

ODYSSEUS And now I promise Teucer that in future
I will be as much a friend as I was once
An enemy. I would also like to take part
In the dead man's burial, leaving no service out
That should be rendered to the best of men.   1380

TEUCER Noble Odysseus, I have only praise for you.
You have wholly belied my expectations.
Of all the Greeks you were his greatest enemy,
Yet you alone came to his aid. You did not dare,
As one of the living, to stand and wrong the dead,   1385
While the demented general and his brother
Were hoping to outrage his body,
And cast him out without a burial.

Teucer and Odysseus

Despite thanking Odysseus, Teucer asks him not to take part in the burial of Ajax for fear of offending the dead man's spirit. The tradition that Ajax's hatred of Odysseus lasted beyond death is found in Homer, *Odyssey xi*. Odysseus enters the world of the dead and finds the spirit of Ajax still implacable.

● Is Teucer's rejection of Odysseus' help ungrateful, or is it simply a part of his duty to his dead kinsman?

1404–5 Others put a tripod over the fire / To receive the holy water
A tripod was placed above a fire to warm the holy water used to wash the body. The body would then be anointed with scents before being buried or cremated (see note on Funeral rites, page 84).

The ending of the play

In his final speech (1402–15) Teucer issues instructions for the burial ceremony. The fact that the speech is in lyric metre and a marching rhythm not only re-emphasises the martial context, but lends an air of solemnity to the end of the play.

In the closing moments attention is focused on the body of Ajax with Eurysaces kneeling beside it. Teucer reaffirms Ajax's greatness (1415), echoing Odysseus' earlier judgement (1340). It is not clear whether Tecmessa is meant to be present in the closing moments of the play.

● Does the action of the play support Teucer's verdict that Ajax was **good in every way**?
● Is this tableau of son and half-brother burying the dead hero a fitting end to the play?

Tragedies often end with a brief conclusion by the Chorus. The tone of the last three lines (1416–18) is similar to Athena's pronouncement on human mortality in 128–33 (see also note on 1359). But whereas Athena warns Odysseus about how gods control human affairs, the Chorus simply conclude that life is unpredictable and the future unknowable.

For that, may the great father of Olympus,
The mindful Fury, and almighty Justice   1:
Destroy those evil men with evil, just as they
Sought to cast out Ajax in undeserved disgrace.
But, son of old Laertes, I am loath
To let you touch the grave, in case it brings
Displeasure to the dead. Still, take part   1395
In all but this and, if you like, bring others
From the army; we will not mind. I shall arrange
Everything else that must be done.
But know that you have been noble to us.

ODYSSEUS I would have liked to be involved, but if you   1400
    Think otherwise, I will go; I respect your wishes.

TEUCER   We have lost enough time already.
          Quickly, some of you dig a hollow grave.
           Others put a tripod over the fire
             To receive the holy water.   1405
           Let others go to his tent and fetch
           His body armour. Now, boy, lift up
           Your father carefully. Help me move
           His body as best you can. His warm
             Veins are still oozing dark blood.   1410
           Come, let all who claim to be here
           As friends be quick to assist a man
             Who was good in every way.
             You could not, while he lived,
           Have served a nobler man than Ajax.   1415

CHORUS   Mortals can fathom many things once seen.
           But nobody, before he sees, can tell
           How he will fare in what is yet to come.

Synopsis of the play

PROLOGUE (1–133)
Odysseus is alone on stage searching for signs of Ajax. Athena appears and tells Odysseus that Ajax has slaughtered the cattle, believing them to be Greek soldiers. She then calls Ajax out from his tent and shows him to Odysseus as a man possessed (Ajax cannot see Odysseus). Ajax retires and, after a brief reflection on human mortality, Odysseus and Athena depart.

PARODOS (134–200)
The Chorus (followers of Ajax) enter. They express their concern at the rumours about Ajax slaughtering cattle, speculate about the cause of his actions, and urge him to defend his good name.

FIRST EPISODE (201–595)
Tecmessa emerges from Ajax's tent and informs the Chorus that their worst fears are true. After this, Ajax appears again, sane this time. He expresses anger at the Greek leaders and despair in the face of his shameful crime. Tecmessa pleads with him to show humility and good sense, but he is intent on dying, and returns to his tent.

FIRST CHORAL ODE (596–645)
The Chorus sing lyrics in which they think of their homeland of Salamis, lament their harsh fate at Troy, and express despair at Ajax's plight.

SECOND EPISODE (646–92)
Ajax re-enters and announces a change of heart. He says that he will purge himself of his offence, and declares that from now on he will yield to the gods and to the Greek leaders. He assures the Chorus that his troubles will soon be over and departs alone.

SECOND CHORAL ODE (693–718)
The Chorus sing a song of jubilation to celebrate Ajax's apparent change of heart.

THIRD EPISODE (719–814)
A messenger arrives from the headquarters of the Greek camp with news of Teucer's return. He describes the hostile reception Teucer received from the Greek army, and recounts the warning from the prophet Calchas that Ajax must not be allowed to depart from his tent

if he is to be seen alive again. Tecmessa, informed of this distressing news, organises a search, and she and the Chorus depart at once.

Scene change
There now follows a change of scene from Ajax's tent to a secluded spot beside the shore, not far from the Greek camp.

FOURTH EPISODE (815–65)
Ajax is alone, with the sword he was given by Hector planted in the earth in front of him. He makes a final speech, before falling on the sword.

FIFTH EPISODE (866–1184)
The Chorus re-enter, still searching for Ajax, and express their frustration at not being able to find him. They hear a cry of despair and find Tecmessa, who has discovered Ajax's body moments after his death but will not permit them to see it. She sings a defiant lament for Ajax. After this Teucer arrives and, upon learning what has happened, he too laments Ajax's death and its likely consequences. Menelaus now appears and demands that Teucer leave Ajax's body unburied. A quarrel takes place between Menelaus and Teucer, but proves inconclusive. Menelaus departs, threatening to muster greater force, and Teucer rushes off to make a tomb. Meanwhile, Tecmessa and Eurysaces arrive to attend Ajax's body.

THIRD CHORAL ODE (1185–1222)
The Chorus again lament their miserable fate at Troy, and deliver a condemnation of war. The ode ends with them once again expressing the desire to be back home on Salamis.

EXODOS (1223–1418)
Teucer returns, closely followed by Agamemnon. Another round of bitter quarrelling ensues, and reaches the point where violence seems inevitable. At this moment, Odysseus arrives and makes peace. He persuades Agamemnon to allow Ajax to be buried and, although there is no love lost between Teucer and Agamemnon, the latter departs. Teucer thanks Odysseus, who also departs. The play ends with Teucer carrying out Ajax's final burial rites along with Eurysaces and the Chorus (Tecmessa may also be present).

Pronunciation of names

To attempt an authentic pronunciation of classical Greek names
presents great difficulties. It is perhaps easiest to accept the
conventional anglicised versions of the familiar names (e.g. Ajax,
Zeus). The key below offers help with all the names in the play, which
will give a reasonable overall consistency. Note that the stress occurs
on the italicised syllable.

> **KEY**
> ay – as in 'hay' ch – as in Scottish 'loch'
> $\bar{e}$ – as in 'hair' $\bar{i}$ – as in 'die'
> $\bar{o}$ – long 'o', as in 'go'

Achaeans	A-*chee*-ans	Knossian	K*noss*-i-an
Achilles	A-*chil*-lees	Laertes	Lay-*er*-tees
Aeacus	*Ee*-a-kus	Laomedon	Lay-*o*-me-dōn
Aegean	Ee-*gee*-an	Menelaus	Me-ne-*lay*-us
Agamemnon	A-ga-*mem*-nōn	Mysia	*Mi*-si-a
Ajax	*Ay*-jax	Odysseus	O-*dis*-se-us
Bosporus	*Bos*-po-rus	Olympus	O-*lim*-pus
Calchas	*Kal*-chas	Pallas	*Pal*-las
Cretan	*Kree*-tan	Pan	Pan
Cyllene	Ki-*lē*-nē	Pelops	*Pe*-lops
Delos	*Dee*-los	Phrygian	*Fri*-ji-an
Erechtheus	E-*rech*-the-us	Salamis	*Sa*-la-mis
Eriboea	E-ri-*bee*-a	Scamander	Ska-*man*-der
Etruscan	E-*trus*-can	Sisyphus	*Si*-si-fus
Eurysaces	Iu-*ri*-sa-kees	Spartan	*Spar*-tan
Hades	*Hay*-dees	Sunium	*Soo*-ni-um
Hector	*Hek*-tōr	Tecmessa	Tek-*mes*-sa
Helios	*Hee*-li-os	Telamon	Te-la-*mōn*
Heracles	*Hee*-ra-klees	Teleutas	Te-*lyoo*-tas
Hermes	*Her*-mees	Teucer	*Tyoo*-ser
Icarian	I-*ka*-ri-an	Thestor	*Thes*-tōr
Ida	*Ī*-da	Zeus	Zyoos

Introduction to the Greek Theatre

Theātron, the Greek word that gave us 'theatre' in English, meant both 'viewing place' and the assembled viewers. These ancient viewers (*theātai*) were in some ways very different from their modern counterparts. For a start, they were participants in a religious festival, and they went to watch plays only on certain days in the year, when shows were put on in honour of Dionysus. At Athens, where drama developed many of its most significant traditions, the main Dionysus festival, held in the spring, was one of the most important events in the city's calendar, attracting large numbers of citizens and visitors from elsewhere in the Greek world. It is not known for certain whether women attended; if any did, they were more likely to be visitors than the wives of Athenian citizens.

The festival was also a great sporting occasion. Performances designed to win the god's favour needed spectators to witness and share in the event, just as the athletic contests did at Olympia or Delphi, and one of the ways in which the spectators got involved was through competition. What they saw were three sets of three tragedies plus a satyr play, five separate comedies and as many as twenty song-and-dance performances called dithyrambs, put on in honour of Dionysus by choruses representing the different 'tribes' into which the citizen body was divided. There was a contest for each different event, with the dithyramb choruses divided into men's and boys' competitions, and a panel of judges determined the winners. The judges were appointed to act on behalf of the city; no doubt they took some notice of the way the audience responded on each occasion. Attendance at these events was on a large scale: we should be thinking of football crowds rather than typical theatre audiences in the modern world.

Like football matches, dramatic festivals were open-air occasions, and the performances were put on in daylight rather than with stage lighting in a darkened auditorium. The ideal performance space in these circumstances was a hollow hillside to seat spectators, with a flat area at the bottom (*orchēstra*) in which the chorusmen could spread out for their dancing and singing and which could be closed off by a stage-building (*skēnē*) acting simultaneously as backdrop, changing room and sounding board. Effective acoustics and good sight-lines were achieved by the kind of design represented in Fig. A on page 106, the theatre of Dionysus at Athens. The famous stone theatre at Epidaurus (Fig. B), built about 330 BC, and often taken as typical, has a circular *orchēstra*, but in the fifth century it was normal

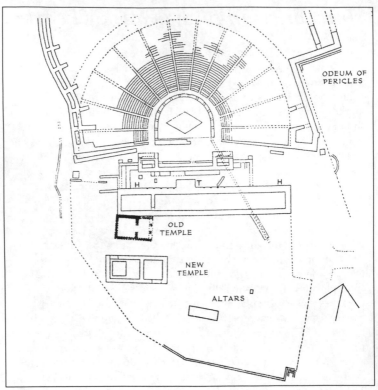

Fig A. The theatre of Dionysus at Athens.

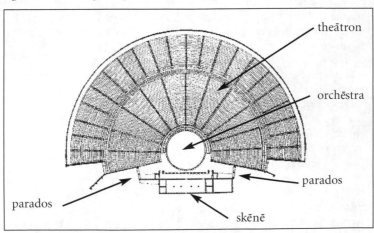

Fig B. The theatre at Epidaurus (fourth century BC).

practice for theatres to have a low wooden stage in front of the *skēne*, for use by the actors, who also interacted with the chorus in the *orchēstra*.

Song and dance by choruses and the accompanying music of the piper were integral to all these types of performance and not just to the dithyramb. In tragedy there were 12 (later 15) chorusmen, in comedy 24, and in dithyramb 50; plays were often named after their chorus: Aeschylus' *Persians*, Euripides' *Bacchae*, Aristophanes' *Birds* are familiar examples. The rhythmic movements, groupings and singing of the chorus contributed crucially to the overall impact of each show, ensuring that there was always an animated stage picture even when only one or two actors were in view. The practice of keeping the number of speaking actors normally restricted to three, with doubling of roles by the same actor where necessary, looks odd at first sight, but it makes sense in the special circumstance of Greek theatrical performance. Two factors are particularly relevant: first the use of masks, which was probably felt to be fundamental to shows associated with the cult of Dionysus and which made it easy for an actor to take more than one part within a single play; and second, the need to concentrate the audience's attention by keeping the number of possible speakers limited. In a large open acting area some kind of focusing device is important if the spectators are always to be sure where to direct their gaze. The Greek plays that have survived, particularly the tragedies, are extremely economical in their design, with no sub-plots or complications in the action which audiences might find distracting or confusing. Acting style, too, seems to have relied on large gestures and avoidance of fussy detail; we know from the size of some of the surviving theatres that many spectators would be sitting too far away to catch small-scale gestures or stage business. Some plays make powerful use of props, like Ajax's sword, Philoctetes' bow, or the head of Pentheus in *Bacchae*, but all these are carefully chosen to be easily seen and interpreted.

Above all, actors seem to have depended on their highly trained voices in order to captivate audiences and stir their emotions. By the middle of the fifth century there was a prize for the best actor in the tragic competition, as well as for the playwright and the financial sponsor of the performance (*chorēgos*), and comedy followed suit a little later. What was most admired in the leading actors who were entitled to compete for this prize was the ability to play a series of different and very demanding parts in a single day and to be a brilliant singer as well as a compelling speaker of verse: many of the main parts involve solo songs or complex exchanges between actor and chorus. Overall, the best plays and performances must have offered audiences a great charge of energy and excitement: the chance to see a group of chorusmen dancing and singing in a sequence of different guises, as young maidens, old counsellors, ecstatic maenads and exuberant satyrs; to watch scenes in which supernatural beings – gods, Furies, ghosts – come into contact with human beings; to listen to intense debates and hear the blood-curdling offstage cries that heralded the arrival of a messenger with an account of terrifying deeds within, and then to see the bodies brought out and witness the lamentations. Far more 'happened' in most plays than we can easily imagine from the bare text on the page; this must help to account for the continuing appeal of drama throughout antiquity and across the Greco-Roman world.

From the fourth century onwards dramatic festivals became popular wherever there were communities of Greek speakers, and other gods besides Dionysus were honoured with performances of plays. Actors, dancers and musicians organised themselves for professional touring – some of them achieved star status and earned huge fees – and famous old plays were revived as part of the repertoire. Some of the plays that had been first performed for Athenian citizens in the fifth century became classics for very different audiences – women as well as men, Latin speakers as well as Greeks – and took on new kinds of meaning in their new environment. But theatre was very far from being an antiquarian institution: new plays, new dramatic forms like mime and pantomime, changes in theatre design, staging, masks and costumes all demonstrate its continuing vitality in the Hellenistic and Roman periods. Nearly all the Greek plays that have survived into modern times are ones that had a long theatrical life in antiquity; this perhaps helps to explain why modern actors, directors and audiences have been able to rediscover their power.

For further reading: entries in *Oxford Classical Dictionary* (3rd edition) under 'theatre staging, Greek' and 'tragedy, Greek'; J.R. Green, 'The theatre', Ch. 7 of *The Cambridge Ancient History, Plates to Volumes V and VI*, Cambridge, 1994; Richard Green and Eric Handley, *Images of the Greek Theatre*, London, 1995; Rush Rehm, *Greek Tragic Theatre*, London and New York, 1992; P.E. Easterling (ed.), *The Cambridge Companion to Greek Tragedy*, Cambridge, 1997; David Wiles, *Tragedy in Athens*, Cambridge, 1997.

Pat Easterling

Time line

Dates of selected authors and extant works

12th Century BC	The Trojan war	
8th Century BC	**HOMER**	• *The Iliad* • *The Odyssey*
5th Century BC 490–479 431–404	**The Persian wars** **The Peloponnesian wars**	

c. 525/4–456/5
 	
472
 	
456
 	
	AESCHYLUS	(In possible order.)
		
		• *Persians*
		• *Seven against Thebes*
		• *Suppliants*
		• **Oresteia Trilogy**:
		   Agamemnon, Choephoroi
		   Eumenides
		• *Prometheus Bound*

c. 496/5–406 409 401 (posthumous)	**SOPHOCLES**	(Undated plays are in alphabetical order.) • *Ajax* • *Oedipus Tyrannus* • *Antigone* • *Trachiniae* • *Electra* • *Philoctetes* • *Oedipus at Colonus*
c. 490/80–407/6 438 (1st production 455) 431 428 415 412 409 ?408 ?408–6 	**EURIPIDES**	(In probable order.) • *Alcestis* • *Medea* • *Heracleidae* • *Hippolytus* • *Andromache* • *Hecuba* • *Suppliant Woman* • *Electra* • *Trojan Women* • *Heracles* • *Iphigenia among the Taurians* • *Helen* • *Ion* • *Phoenissae* • *Orestes* • *Cyclops* (satyr-play) • *Bacchae* • *Iphigenia at Aulis*
460/50–*c.* 386 411 405	**ARISTOPHANES**	(Selected works.) • *Thesmophoriazusae* • *Lysistrata* • *Frogs*
4th Century BC 384–322	**ARISTOTLE**	(Selected works.) • *The Art of Poetry*

Index

Bold numbers refer to pages. Other numbers are line references.

Printed in the United States
By Bookmasters